Other titles by Howard Ingram:

Fiction

Non Fiction

Reminiscences at Sixty

Howard Ingram

authorHOUSE®

AuthorHouse™ UK Ltd.
500 Avebury Boulevard
Central Milton Keynes, MK9 2BE
www.authorhouse.co.uk
Phone: 08001974150

First published by AuthorHouse 9/10/2007

ISBN: 978-1-4343-2520-4 (sc)

Printed in the United States of America
Bloomington, Indiana

This book is printed on acid-free paper.

Dedication

There is one person who makes my life purposeful and joyful

Athena

Preface

Many books of quotations give you a collection of wise and wonderful sayings, which, although grand within themselves, may become somewhat dry as one wades through them and thus become useful as reference only. On attaining the milestone age of 60, I look back at the quotations I have collected over the past 50 years, starting with the very first one, given to me by my father when I was 10 years old:

"Know thyself, accept thyself, be thyself"

No, not Shakespeare, Alexander Pope

Why did I begin this collection of oddities, wisdom and nonsense? Because everything I have collected or created has meant something to me, then as now, and each quotation collected or created shows a moment in my personal development, sometimes happy, sometimes cynical, sometimes sad.

Who is this book directed to?
Encouragement to a ten year old boy to now start making his own collection to see where his life takes him, or perhaps for reflection with a 60 year old friend of where our lives conjoin and where they differ?
Or simply for me and to my wife Athena and our children, Stafford, Nicole, Scott and Russell and their children, too?

It's me, - but it could be you. At least some of it may stir a chord, a memory, or perhaps evoke one. And I am offering it to you not as a dry collection, but as a story. I hope you enjoy....

Howard Cant 20th September 2006 (my 60th birthday)

I

If you can't make it as a great man, at least be a good one

Penned by me on 1st September, the month of my 60th birthday; recognizing that the thoughts of greatness, thoughts that we all had when we were young, become reality to only a few; the highly driven, the ones that make their own luck and those that have the cojones to take the rough with the smooth and not let society or their peers grind them down. Men like Winston Churchill and Bill Clinton and Muhammad Ali and some others, rather few in my lifetime; but so it is in everyone's lifetime.

Apropos nothing at all, and to begin on a rather uncharitable observation, but as I am now sixty, I really am allowed to say whatever I feel; I turned on a television news item yesterday, coming from the US of A and this thought hit me like a physical presence:

Why are the inhabitants of New Orleans so uniformly overweight,
– and so crass and not very beautiful?

I guess they won't be stocking this book. But honestly, they are.

James Cagney, at around about the age of 60, I can't vouch for the exact date, told the world, in one of his rare interviews of becoming modesty:

1

Say what you mean,
And mean what you say

This is what I intend to do in my little book of quotations and reminiscences. If I can't do it now, when I'm sixty, when will I ever? I just hope Jimmy didn't come from New Orleans.

I travelled from Phuket, Thailand to Seoul, Korea two days ago and was sitting in the Business Class lounge of Thai airways. I glanced at the TV screen listing the departures and I was struck by the thought, a thought that may have come to other frequent travellers:

What does it tell you about your past and future life,
When you sit for two hours in a Business Class Lounge
And, looking, for all of that time
At the departures information displayed on the TV monitor;
You do not see one single destination,
That you have not visited.
What does it tell you about your past and future life?

I'm working on a major project during my 60th year and I thought I might share it with you; just to motivate others. The project is to be able to view, once again, from a standing position, an appendage of mine; without having a protruding mass prohibiting it from view. I know it's there, I use it a few times every day, but I can't remember when I last saw it from a standing position. Exercise in earnest tomorrow, Howard. Tonight, I'll just have a small scotch and soda before retiring to bed to ensure the project is placed and sealed in its proper perspective.

'Night all'

Any among you remember the TV actor who, in the early days of BBC Television made that phrase so popular, such a household expression? Ask me if it's driving you daft. A clue; he was the very first TV copper and his name began with 'D'.

One very important thing to remember when you are turning sixty (or maybe at any age, actually) is what dear, sad, wonderful, strong, yet ultimately pathetic Ernest Hemingway told us (in 1923) when we are inclined, often with a morbid curiosity, a beguiling sadness or a wish unfulfilled, to look back on our lives:

> *We can't ever go back to old things or try and get the 'old kick'*
> *out of something or find things the way we remembered them.*
> *We have them as we remember them and they are fine and wonderful*
> *and we have to go on and have other things,*
> *Because the old things are nowhere except in our minds now.*

60 years of age, especially when you live, as I do, in Asia; as I have done for over 25 years and if you are blessed with grey hair, is a fabulous age. Money in your pocket, extraordinary respect given just because you are 'old', as long as you are also reasonably smart: not one of the grossly tummied, frequently unshaven, beer guzzling expats on a fixed income and regarding the talent (male or female) in the bars of Thailand (and elsewhere) as their own cookie jar. Dreadful people, not of the same biological family…. you wish.

> *Would that God had the gift tae gie us*
> *Tae see ourselves as others see us.*

This from the poet and earthy philosopher, Robbie Burns; the greatest of Scottish poets (actually not too many to choose from), and one of my Mother's favourites. Mum was born and brought up in a not very well-off Glasgow family, ultimately living a most fulfilling life as a local Councillor, a Justice of the Peace and as secretary to my father who was in politics, both local and national; sitting as the Labour Member of Parliament for Stoke-on-Trent in England for 30 years, as well as having had a fulfilling previous career as a Senior Lecturer in Economics for Oxford and Keele (Staffordshire) universities. He achieved a double first at the LSE (London School of Economics – some claim it to be an even more prestigious university than either Oxford or Cambridge, especially for Politics, Philosophy and Economics) just after the Second World War. A war he was invalided out from, with a courageously gained torn cartilage - on the football field! In the Signal Corps he was; thankfully never got over to Germany in action, otherwise I might not be here. Mind you, he was always a tough act to follow, - I never paralleled his intelligence quotient, but I did have other things about me that, in time, he came to appreciate and respect. That's a great moment for a son to experience, when your Dad says; 'I really respect you, son.' What was it that Mark Twain had to say? Ah yes….

When I was fourteen, I thought my father the most stupid man in the world. When I reached twenty-one, I was amazed at how much he had learned in six years

Sadly, however, many sons feel of their father much the same as Peter Ustinov recollects in his autobiography, 'Dear Me', recording on the demise of this parent:

So vanished a man I never really knew, and whom I, like all sons everywhere, needed to know better. There is no fault attached to this. The need and awkwardness lie somewhere deep in human nature. The cross-currents of jealousy, of ambition, of protectiveness, of authority try and work under the level of consciousness however well they are controlled by breeding and usage.

His father's dying words to Peter were:

I recognise you from my dreams

If those words were said to me in such a situation, they would forever haunt me.

For most of the past 10 years, I've lived in Thailand. I retired to Cyprus from Singapore when I was in my late 40's, did many of the things I'd always wanted to do and that business had kept me away from. I acted in Shakespeare productions in a 3,000 seater Greco Roman Amphitheatre in Episkopi, Cyprus. Not before I had re-read and wondered, somewhat uneasily, about what that great character actor, Sir Ralph Richardson (1902-1983) had to say about his chosen profession:

Acting is merely the art of keeping a large group of people from coughing

A thought also rather keenly felt by William Boyd Gatewood (a not too well known author) when he declared in or around 1915:

> *Very few people go to the doctor when they have*
> *a cold. They go to the theatre instead*

Not a lot's changed in some respects in almost 100 years.

John Barrymore, not everyone's favourite as an actor, or even as a person, had a gift, denied to many of us, of being able, succinctly, albeit often crudely, to exactly identify something about the theatre and the art of acting that pass by many calmer souls. As quoted in Anthony Quinn's Autobiography, 'The Original Sin', Barrymore was heard to proclaim:

> *Anybody can make shit out of beauty; it takes*
> *great courage to make beauty out of shit*

Not just an acting analogy, I feel. To achieve this takes good direction, but it is a truism, worth reflecting on, that no matter what a director may wish to aspire to, at the end of the day, as Martin Esslin in 'The signs of drama' would have us remember:

> *The actor is the essential ingredient around which all drama revolves.*
> *There can be, and there has been, drama without writers, designers,*
> *directors*
> *– there can never be drama without actors*

Our dreams of retirement in the sunny island of Cyprus soon waned as we became bored with the same food, poor wine and frequent impoliteness of the Cypriots, - but most of all we hated the 'hunting mentality' of grown men, dressing up in fatigues and shooting poor pretty little birds and thinking that all that was macho. But perhaps many of us Brits are, or have been just as bad; as Oscar Wilde put it:

The English country gentleman,
Galloping after a fox,
The unspeakable,
In pursuit of the inedible

So we left Cyprus; not before I was lucky enough to do Sir Toby in Twelfth Night and both twins (simultaneously) in 'A Comedy of Errors'; chasing myself on and off the stage, racing round backstage to put on a different coat and hat and emerging as the 'other' Antipholus. Both plays ably directed by Colin Garland. But, for me, the best performance of my acting career came as John Proctor in 'The Crucible'. I did a bit of Pinter too, perhaps more correctly, he did me. I know he is a brilliant writer, but, I sometimes feel, a rather sad and incomplete man, especially when he proclaims:

> *No matter how you look at it, all the emotions connected with love are not really immortal; like all other passions in life, they are bound to fade at some point. The trick is to convert love into some lasting friendship that overcomes the fading passion*

So, back to the Far East for Athena and me; in our hearts we had never left. We settled in Phuket, we attempted to learn Thai; I did an Open University degree in English, History and the History of Art, then Athena needed to get me from under her feet, so I went back to work at the age of 55. I've done my retirement, loved it, may decide never to retire again; need to keep the brain active and the hand away from the lunch-time gins, which soon waste the entire day for so many retirees. But I still frequently walk on the beach with our dogs, in the early morning as the sun comes up. I penned this recollection on one such walk in January 2000, thoughts still as vivid today;

The beginning of the day

One of the most glorious, intimate ways in which to begin the day is to sit on a sweet sandy beach, with rollers bashing in. Gentle but bashing; watching, under shaded eyes against the brilliant early morning sun, a young, scantily clad girl, buttocks exposed, gamboling in the shallows with a dog. Tease and double tease.

6

And to know, – best of all,
That,
It is <u>your</u> dog!

Returning to Asia in 1998 was like coming home. In reality we hadn't been away too long, only since 1994 when we exited the sterility of Singapore, having spent a not too happy four year spell there; except for the sailboats we'd owned and the escapes they had given us as we journeyed around Singapore, with excursions into Indonesia, Malaysia and Thailand. Our last boat was a 43 foot Beneteau Oceanis and we loved it. Just the two of us, sailing to Rawa island in Malaysia, with dolphins playing at the prow all through the night. Athena and I are incompatible in (at least) one respect. I like retiring to bed anytime between 10 and 11p.m., she doesn't think about sleeping until way past midnight. So, it's great on a boat; she takes the 11p.m. to 4 or 5 a.m. watch and I take the early morning, which I love the best. But as any serious boat owner will tell you:

The two most pleasurable days in boat ownership
Are the day you buy, and the day you sell

Leaving the boat one day and walking along the beach I saw two wondrous sights. The first was a large Thai lady on her motor scooter with a gorgeously full head of hair and a monkey sitting right on top of her head, picking at that gloriousness; then I saw, striding most purposefully along the beach, a very stern, bespectacled, young, almost breast-less Thai woman, with the following message blazing forth from her tiny T-shirted bosom:

Most people should be sterilized

I felt great empathy with her message. My thoughts were specifically directed, they came soon after 9/11.

Sir Peter Ustinov, who died in 2004 at the age of 83, lived in a world where it was said that he could 'make anyone laugh', but there was a serious side to his soul that gave us many opportunities to reflect upon the mad extremism of our world and its abrasive religions and cultures:

No extreme fascinates me. I think it's all wrong because it's all too
easy. These louts, anarchists or whatever they are, who go out into
the streets to riot and break windows, don't have to think anymore.
They're following instructions. Well, that's easy. And the storm-
troopers I saw in Germany as a boy, all shouting 'Germany Awake!'
It gives them a sense of communal core, and there's nothing more
exhilarating for a certain clot-like mentality, than the sound of
boots marching all together, 'and you're part-of-the-machine-and-
it's-wonderful'. In point of fact, it's the isolated voice which can't
even be heard in the crowd, which is really the most vital of all.

Even perhaps too simplistic, today, Sir Peter; with the absolutely careless barbarism and terror of Al Qaeda and the like. I sometimes feel that:

The only global movement worthy of financial support is that of
providing funding for the sterilization of extremist Muslims

But how to find them and differentiate them from the not-quite-so-extreme Muslims?

I'm sorry if that statement incites you. But I suggest, it should only do so if you are yourself an extremist, thus proving the truth inherent in the quotation.
Maybe I should talk with the girl in the T-shirt!

When you reach the age of 60 and you live abroad in a warm and unregimented environment, you look at the England of today and compare with the England you remember as a youth. It gives rise to thoughts such as I experienced when in England on Boxing Day, 2001:

England now, is a prison for me,
Its jailors are…
Television and Cold and Foreigners and Darkness

8

And, – Family and Haste and Pressure.
England now is a prison for me.

England has lost its manners, relinquished its mannerisms,
Its identity.
England now is purely a geographical term.
Patriotism survives but little, in pockets.
In the Establishment, in the Castles and in the Creeds,
Of the Monarchy

It does not survive in its Parliament,
The Mother of all Parliaments

Englishness is dead, – or almost dead.

The Young, the Immigrants, the Thrusters,
The Takers, the Unmannered, the Slothful,
Idle, Hopeless, probably think,
If they think at all,
That it is a good thing.
Good?
Goodbye.
Simply Goodbye!
Oh England!
To England!

Maybe Enoch Powell, that distinguished and greatly controversial British Statesman (much more than a politician), who died from Parkinson's disease in 1998 at the age of 85, may have said it better:

England is a stage on which the drama of English history was
played and the setting within which the English became conscious of
themselves as a people…when politicians and preachers attempt to
frighten and cajole the English into pretending away the distinction
between themselves and people of other nations and other origins,
they are engaged in undermining the foundation upon which
democratic government by consent and peaceable civilized society
in this country are supported. Those who at the end of the twentieth

century wish to keep alive the consciousness of being English, which seemed so effortless and uncontroversial to our forefathers, will discover that they are called upon, if they take their purpose seriously, to confront the most arrogant and imposing prejudices of their time.

Not all of my quotations are so heavy. Have a drink!

II

Sir Arthur Helps, sometime confidant of Queen Victoria who entrusted him with preparing an appreciation of her husband's life and character; so she must have trusted his perspicacity; lived from 1813 to 1875. He penned two plays, 'King Henry the Second' and 'Catherine Douglas'. Neither in these, nor in his only other dramatic effort, 'Oulita the Serf' (1858) did he display any real qualifications as a playwright. He had a few good friends, some at court, but he was also smart enough to recognise, as some of us might, that:

People speak of the sadness of being in a crowd and knowing no-one. There is something pleasurable in it too

Friendships are dramatically important to one's development; both as a maturing person and as a caring individual, especially when making a new country one's home. I don't have many friendships; I wonder what that says about me. Actually, I can only think of a couple of *real* friends, the ones that you look forward to staying in your house for more than 24 hours continuously. The ones that don't become like fish. You know, go off after only two days. The ones you want to chat to, to debate with, to become comfortably inebriated with. Only one or two for me. Richard Davenport-Hines writing a biography of the Macmillan family put it thus:

Friendships should be the study of every biographer. The way a man relates to other people and chooses attachments is as eloquent of character as anything else

What is it that is the mainstay of friendship? Is it commonality or even contrast of ideas? Is it a shared secret? I rather believe, with Oscar Wilde, that:

*Ultimately the bond of all companionship, whether
in marriage or in friendship, is conversation*

Obviously, we want our friends and acquaintances to respect and to like us, as J. Petit-Senn perceptively pointed out:

It is almost impossible to find those who admire us lacking in taste

Relating to other people can become compellingly eloquent through body language, especially body language displayed by the subconscious copying of the stance and behaviour of others; body language that may sometimes form a remarkable empathy because it is immediately and unconsciously copied from the company of another person. EM Forster in 'A Room with a View' put it thus:

*She stopped and leant her elbows against the parapet of the embankment.
He did likewise. There is at times a magic in identity of position;
it is one of the things that have suggested to us eternal comradeship*

For me, however, many of the great friendships of the world have not always occurred between humans. I rather like James Herriott's friend Cedric in 'All Things Wise and Wonderful':

*You couldn't help liking Cedric when you got to know him. He was
utterly amiable and without vice and he gave off a constant aura not
merely of noxious vapours but of bonhomie. When he tore off people's
buttons or sprinkled their trousers,
he did it in a spirit of the purest amity.*

I truly relate to why Tom Hanks, in the film 'Castaway' was distraught and devastated as he lost his companion overboard when escaping from the island that had contained them for so long. His companion had been a football, to whom he had given life and personality, a face and a character. A companion who had sustained him in the dark days and nights of his isolation. A companion with whom he spoke and shared his fears, his successes, his failures. To have lost him, at that juncture, just when he was in reach of being saved, was more heartbreaking than many a human loss.

Maybe it's a terrible admission, but I'm 60 and I can look at myself and my feelings totally honestly and I know that:

I can dispassionately watch the TV news and see men killing women and children and each other in Iraq, in Palestine, in Africa and feel nothing. I watch as an animal, wild or tame, is being maltreated and I feel fury.

Recently, I read an odd little book by Misha Defonseca called 'Surviving with wolves'. It is her account of the time when, as a young and terribly lonely seven year old child during the ravages of the Second World War in Europe, she lived with wolves as her only family, as she trekked across Belgium, Germany, Poland and the Ukraine:

I can still see that magnificent creature (the wolf that befriended her, but was shot and killed by a hunter) *hanging from a hook. Years later, I thought, 'What men do to animals, they're also prepared to do to humans; they hang people in the same way. Man is the despicable predator of the world. He has learned nothing. He is destroying a beautiful world because he's jealous of it. He is destroying animals because he cannot run as fast as they do, because he doesn't have such a keen sense of smell and cannot hear as acutely. He's jealous of the trees, which are tall and lovely. Man is colourless.
He is full of vice. How can I be a human being? It's impossible.
I've never been able to cure myself of thoughts like that.*

But not all animals are loveable, which brings us to Jones's goat and, as this is a rather lengthy quotation, I would like to recommend a G&T or whatever your favourite tipple might be to enjoy it to the full. The quotation comes from Laurie Lee's autobiography of his childhood years – 'Cider with Rosie':

But there was one real old pagan of flesh and
blood who ruled us all for a while.
I had fallen half asleep across the table,
when Marjorie suddenly said, 'Ssssh!'
Then Dorothy said, 'Hark!'
and Mother said, 'Hush!' and the alarm had us all in its grip.
Like a stagless herd of hinds and young our heads all went up together.
We heard it then, faraway down the lane, still faint and unmistakable
– the drag of metal on frosty ground and
an intermittent rattle of chains.
The drag of the chains grew louder and nearer, rattling along the night,
sliding towards us up the distant lane to his remorseless, moonlit tread.
'Jones's goat!' – our Dorothy whispered; two words that were almost
worship. For this was not just a straying animal but a beast of ancient
dream, the moonlight walker of the village roads, half captive, half
rutting King. He was huge and hairy as a Shetland horse and all
men were afraid of him. Daughters and wives peeped from darkened
bedrooms, men waited in the shadows with axes. Meanwhile, reeking
with power and white in the moon, he went his awesome way....
'Did you ever see a goat so big?' asked Dorothy with a sigh.
'Just think of meeting him coming home alone...'
'Whatever would you do?'
'I'd have a fit. What would you do Phyl?'
Phyl didn't answer: she had run away, and
was having hysterics in the pantry.

I just love his descriptive writing capacity. Life is made up of the facility we have to recognise ability, even genius and, if we can avoid being jealous of something we don't ourselves possess, then we can truly relish it.

How do we follow Jones's goat? Maybe with one's own list of 'goats' - of the human variety. Who would you put into *your* goat book? – Powerful, scary, rutting, stupid? On second thoughts, perhaps a goat is not so stupid, not like a sheep. Anyway, in my goat book I'd probably put Picasso; he drew some pretty scary stuff, was a powerful force both as a person and in the art world, and certainly did more than his share of rutting. Ernest Hemingway would also be in my book, although he'd probably have shot anybody who called him a goat, but I think he fits the bill; as does one of the greatest rutters of all time; JFK. A splendid White House Rutter, but also a scary politician and, indisputably powerful. There have been successors in that White place, but never as competent nor as frequently goatish as he. As Mae West said, obviously thinking of rutting:

Too much of a good thing is.....wonderful!

I wonder how many of us would have enjoyed meeting and being with Mae West? I feel to do so would necessitate a person of sexual erudition somewhat beyond the norm, especially when we remember her most famous quote:

Is that a gun in your pocket, or are you just happy to see me?

Whatever she did and however she lived her life, she managed it to be a long and interesting one, dying at the age of 87 in 1980

One of the most controversial stars of her day, Mae West encountered many obstacles, including early censorship and sexism. I wonder how much of a soul mate she would have found in Oscar, especially when he said:

I can resist anything except temptation

It could have come from either of them, don't you agree?

III

I've spent one and a half years now in Korea, having the doubtful accolade of being the only Western CEO of a wholly Korean owned company – the Young In Group; at this moment consisting of 5 companies, whose activities range from importing and distributing scientific instruments to manufacturing the same or similar and to creating antibodies for research that may, one day, eradicate the terrible diseases of Alzheimer's, Parkinson's and Cancer. Experiencing prolonged periods – frequently three weeks - away from my wife, Athena, makes the passage below even more poignant, in a world gone mad with Islamic extremists, where no one's wife is safe, nor those inhabiting the used-to-be pure world of children and childhood. I found it in the autobiography of Sheila Hancock and John Thaw, written by her on his death at the age of 60, dead of cancer. At the time he was the most famous actor on British TV. The book is a sometimes difficult but outstandingly real read. Sheila was sent the passage by a well-wisher after John's death, when she was simply unable to bear the grief. The passage originates in 'The Smoke Jumper' by Nicholas Evans. It goes…

If I be the first of us to die,
Let grief not blacken long your sky.
Be bold yet modest in your grieving.
There is change but not a leaving.
For just as death is part of life,
The dead live on forever in the living.

Beautiful though tough, yet sustaining; reminiscent at times of Shakespeare's songs or sonnets. Not, however, to be read when you are alone and have had one glass too many. I challenge the toughest amongst us not to.......

At this moment, just as I had typed that quotation on my laptop, I opened a page of one of my collections and found an old Irish proverb, the page just opened at it, honestly. What a positive balance it offers to the previous quotation and a challenging legitimacy:

Dance as if no-one is watching,
Sing as if no one's listening
And live every day as if it were your last

Go on, bloody do it!

And remember, when you're dancing in front of anyone, the quotation from Samuel Johnson, writing in the mid 18th Century:

The true measure of a man is how he treats someone
who can do him absolutely no good

When Athena and I came 'home' to Phuket we rented a delightful small one story house with a large untamed garden. There was no hot water in the house; no-one had ever thought that hot water was necessary in such a warm climate. – The house was at least 15 years old and had done very nicely without it, thank you very much. But warm water, courtesy of admonitions from Athena, was installed shortly after our arrival there. Greasy dishes and greasy bodies respond better to hot than cold water, to that I can attest. But it did seem, at the time, that I was giving in to something I really didn't want to give in to.

Our nearest neighbour was a strikingly tall, black American named Ted, who had once been a cop on the beat, probably in one of the most difficult cities in America. An LAPD style of individual if ever there was one. We never truly discovered where he had practiced his profession, he didn't communicate much. Rather, he simply lay in his hammock for much of the day, from time to time raising himself to create a wonderland of stuffed or ceramic and bronze animals, complete with extensive fairy lights, throughout his 'estate'. There were monkeys climbing trees, giraffes drinking from make-believe streams (concrete across the width of his garden, painted blue), tigers preparing to pounce and all nature of fowls sitting and swooping. He could make anything out of a coconut, and frequently did. Then he painted it pink, or red, or orange, or blue, or whatever. You didn't mess with Ted:

Black Ted

Black Ted is seventy-four years old
They call Ted, 'Black Ted',
Because he is,
Black.

Ted, resting in his hammock all day,
Or painting,
Has had his life.

But he has a better one now.
Life, that is.
Ted is gentle, friendly but not familiar,
Unfamiliarly friendly;
Black Ted.

Ted needs his own space.
Black Ted is gentle, but perhaps,
Sometimes,
Not kind.
Ted needs his own space
And,
He takes it.

Neighbours can be great objects of fun and discussion, of hate and of love; of assistance and of distress. We all remember the good ones and the bad ones. Laurie Lee (again, - he's just so good) in his autobiography, 'Cider with Rosie', introduced us to some of his:

From the age of five or so I began to grow acquainted with several neighbours – outlaws most of them in dress and behaviour – whom I remember both by name and deed. There was Cabbage-Stump Charlie, Albert the Devil and Percy-from-Painswick, to begin with. Cabbage-Stump Charlie was our local bruiser, - a violent, gaitered, gaunt-faced pigman, who lived only for his sows and for fighting. He was a nourisher of quarrels, as some men are of plants, growing them from nothing by the heat of belligerence and working them daily with blood. He would set out each evening, armed with his cabbage stalk, ready to strike down the first man he saw. 'What's up then, Charlie? Got no quarrel with thee.' 'Wham!' said Charlie, and hit him. Men fell from their bicycles or back-pedalled violently when they saw old Charlie coming. With his hawk-brown nose and whiskered arms he looked like a land-locked Viking; and he would take up his stand outside the pub, swing his great stump round his head and say, 'Wham! Bash!' like a boy in a comic, and challenge all comers to battle. Often bloodied himself, he left many a man bleeding before crawling back home to his pigs. Cabbage-Stump Charlie, like Jones's goat, set the village to bolting its doors.

Now, this small house of ours in Phuket with its one-off neighbour had, as I mentioned before, a substantial garden, untamed; that we in our wisdom decided to tame. So, we went about it with vigour; more vigour than craft and, after straining the odd back here and cutting fingers on thorns there, I came to the unoriginal conclusion that what we needed was a gardener. So, as it always is in Thailand, once the requirement is mentioned to anyone Thai, up one sprung within nanoseconds, who, working as he was at The Royal Meridian Yacht Club just down the road, was willing to come, once every week on his day off, for the princely sum of 1,500 Baht, or about 40 US dollars per month, ten per day. I still have him and he now works for us in our second home in Phuket, which has a much smaller garden, but today he enjoys the exorbitant salary of 2,500 Baht or about 63 US dollars a month. Where did I go wrong?

Actually, he wasn't our first gardener, but the first guy lasted one month only; so I disregarded him in this narrative, although, the following was penned in his honour in November 1999:

I have a gardener,
Who has mastered,
Lethargy
He is the envy of cats.
It takes my gardener,
More than,
Five minutes
To work up to having;
A contemplative cigarette
The cats admire him.
I have a gardener,
I had

Deep in my memory somewhere, I recall a line from a play:

Please come into my garden, I would like my roses to see you

I can't remember, for the life of me, where it came from, but it does sound rather like Oscar Wilde, or maybe Noel Coward? – If anyone knows, please e-mail me and put me out of my misery. – It's all to do with the memory of a 60 year old, I guess! However, age is purely in the mind of the statisticians; we all remember and those of us sixty plus, remember it best that:

You are only as old as the woman you feel

Hence the activity of many Western geriatrics, especially in Thailand; gosh, they are so often such dire sights. Their families would disown them immediately if they could but see them in their new habitat. However, perhaps James Thurber, writing in 1957, has a most significant point:

I'm sixty-three and I guess that puts me in with the geriatrics.
But if there were fifteen months in every year, I'd be only forty-three

Phuket is an island of endless oddities, some delightful, some less so. Where in that scale do the Ladyboys, the 'Katoeys', come, I wonder? The beautiful boys who want to be and look like beautiful women. Lost forever in a neverland. Pretty, but sad:

There but for the grace of God, go we

But it does rain a hell of a lot here in Phuket. It's not enough to pretend that the rain is 'warm' or 'warmish', it is incredibly tedious; especially when golf is planned, or a nice sit by or in the pool with glass in hand, reading the latest killing machine book, penned by ex-SAS masterful storyteller, Chris Ryan. Who, by the way, I used to think, writes confounded self perpetuating violent rubbish. But now, I've undergone a wonderful metamorphosis and sincerely appreciate his fantastically urgent pace and sheer unrelentingly grabbing pressure. I wonder if he writes standing up. Give me his next book, anytime. BUT, as I said, sitting in the pool, reading novels between the months of July to November in monsoon plagued Phuket, can be a bit iffy. GK Chesterton (1874-1936), larger than life, both physically and mentally, when watching a tremendous rainstorm, alas, not in Phuket, said it thus:

I don't care where the water goes if it doesn't get into the wine

Delightful man and outstanding writer, who was always able to make fun of himself:

I always enjoy myself more than most, there's such a lot of me having a good time

When I was younger, I used to play a game of 'who would you like to meet, if you could meet anyone in the world?' – At first, for me, it was Churchill and Hemingway and Shakespeare and Oscar Wilde, but then I graduated to GK and John Major and Frank Muir. But I never ever, ever, wanted to meet Margaret Thatcher.
Ray Leonard, onetime heavyweight champion of the world was once asked 'Do you want to become a great man?'

*'Man', he says, 'I'm just a fighter. That's all. If you want to
know about greatness, watch Muhammad Ali. Watch people
around Ali. If you put him in a hall of people with Castro and
Gorbachev, everybody'd flock to Ali. That's greatness.'*

CS Lewis must have played this game at some time or another
(perhaps we all do) for, in 1942, he had this to say:

*I would go a long way to meet Beatrice or Falstaff or
Mr. Jonathan Oldbuck or Disraeli's Lord Monmouth.
I would not cross the room to meet Hamlet.
It would never be necessary. He is always where I am.*

It's funny how we change, isn't it? If I were to play the game today,
I'd probably want to meet the unsung heroes and the ones that never
make it into the spotlight. The guys and girls who saved so many lives
in the dreadful Tsunami of 2004, which claimed some of my friends
but from which Athena and I had a lucky escape. – The right place
at the right time for us, but not for so many others.
Yes, that's the type of people I'd now feel privileged to meet.

But John Denver will forever remain on my 'must meet' list.

Sunshine on my shoulders makes me happy

A man who proved in life to be the total antithesis of Oscar's
description of one of his acquaintances;

*He hasn't become prominent enough to have any enemies.
But none of his friends like him.*

No one could ever say that about John Denver, beloved by all, a man
who brought so much real joy through his songs to so many people;
a man wretchedly snatched from this world in 1997. Some others
departing in 1997, not including my father who also died that year,
were, in my opinion, not such a great loss to mankind. Oops!

I guess I've proved OW right again,

We are each our own devil, and we make this world our hell.

Thanks, Oscar.

IV

For those of you willing to open mindedly enjoy the on-going mysteries of the East, there is so much still to learn, to try to understand. But it is really difficult to grasp the essence of some countries or cities no matter how long you live there. We might believe, along with Rupert Brooke, that it is quite pointless to attempt to understand a city during the daytime for:

Cities like cats, will reveal themselves at night

Most of us do our sightseeing during daytime hours and the sadness of so many beautiful cities in our world now is that they share the common grief of night-time menace. There are many fewer cities in the world today that my wife and I can wander around without compunction after ten o clock in the evening than there were in our youth. Sad.

I have had the great good fortune to live in England (now no longer England, - see above!) Hong Kong (loved it), Singapore (too restrictive and robotic and unfriendly), Cyprus (great at first but then waning with repetitiveness and becoming boring), Thailand, (always, always great and surprising and just a little bit more than a little bit crazy, frustrating, challenging, sensuous and fun), and Korea (what does one really say about Korea?) I've lived in Korea for more than one year now, although I frequently visited between 1980 and 1990, when it was such a different place; then there was great poverty, lack of electricity and very little heating except in the hotels; smelly taxis running on gas, rampant prostitution, a great divide between the haves and have nots. Today, however I feel it is:

Clean, generally; everything works, probably the most efficient airport in the world, but too controlled and going the way of Singapore. The people are long on etiquette but short on manners; car, taxi and especially bus drivers are all selfish to the extreme, but maybe they have to be so because of the relentless traffic, both night and day. But the people are so grim, no smiles for the passing stranger, as in Thailand. Everything, everybody is far too serious; there is little evident joy in the land; understandably if you consider its history of occupation and oppression by the Japanese and the communist insurgency of the 1950's.

Then, what about Japan? Shirley Maclaine, in her well written biography 'Don't Fall off the Mountain', tells of the time she spent there with her much loved yet peripatetic husband and daughter;

Japan is a land where time has no urgency, where the important thing is human relations, where friction must be avoided at all costs, and where a highly ritualized sense of courtesy has developed to eliminate it. In Japan, courtesy has an aesthetic value far greater than good manners in the West. A negative truth is frequently subordinate to the virtue of courtesy. Courtesy, therefore, is more of a virtue than honesty.

Are the Koreans and the Japanese very alike? They would claim not to be, but, to the untutored Westerner the similarities are striking and somewhat disturbing. But then, are they also like other races too? Simon Winchester writing of his travels through Korea in the 1980's in his book entitled 'Korea – a walk through the land of miracles' gave us this insight:

'The Koreans are so like the Irish', someone had said to me back in Cheju. 'They're sweet and sentimental. They're sad. They sing songs, and sad songs too. But if you get them angry, you'll be terrified. They have a kind of anger that is unforgettable. They completely lose control of themselves. They've no idea what they are doing. It's a frightening sight. Never make a Korean angry. You'll come off worse if you do'.

I agree, and I've had first-hand experience of this phenomenon. In a somewhat heated business discussion some time ago, the Korean negotiator was becoming increasingly loud and morose; suddenly he stood up, glowered over me for a second, then went to his office door and with a slippered foot, smashed the thick glass in the frame with a tremendous fury filled kick that would have broken a man's back; shattering splinters and wickedly sharp glass daggers all over the floor; then he marched out of the room. Stupefied, nay terrified, I and my companion were speechless. The following day we resumed our negotiations, quietly and politely; the glass had been replaced and we finally concluded the deal. It was astonishing.

Koreans fart in lifts. Actually they fart anywhere, the men, I mean. The worst of all is in a closed car or a lift and it's considered impolite <u>of you</u> if you wind down the window or waft your nose with a bunch of papers!

> *Would that God had the gift tae gie us*
> *To smell ourselves as others smell us*

Sorrie, Robbie.

Yet, in Korea there is a tremendous sense of soul, of sadness, of history; indeed, once outside the city centres, a true sense of concentrated calm and peacefulness. Korea once clung to the epithet of *the land of the morning calm*, the land of mists. Not quite so much today, perhaps, but there is a self-effacing beauty redolent amongst its people who still embody the feelings displayed by their poet Yi Hwang (1501-70):

> *Let my house be morning mists,*
> *And my friends the wind and moon;*
> *While the land is at peace*
> *I'll decline into old age.*
> *Just one thing I ask of life:*
> *That my faults may disappear.*

In complete contrast, I can sum up all that Thailand means to me in the following apparition, seen in Phuket in November 1999:

26

Caught in the headlight beam

Tonight,
Caught in the headlight beam,
Were reflectors

Wrapped around the,
Feet;
Of,
Elephants.

Crossing the road, from left to right.

When
You;
Have seen,
Reflectors on the feet

Of elephants.

What is there left in life to see?

I've spent quite a bit of time in America too, and now to lose my American readers, I must agree with Oscar when he noted:

Of course America had often been discovered before Columbus,
but it had always been hushed up!

We are living in an age of much bad press for America and the Americans, but it is their own fault. I like many individual Americans I have met over the years, but their collective arrogance is mind numbing and in deep contrast to the Asian races. Nelson De Mille, writing in his novel 'The Charm School' had one of his characters say this about the self-proclaimed master race:

It is only since I've had to deal with hundreds of Americans that I've
grown to hate them, hate their culture, their filthy books and magazines,
their shallow motives, their selfish personalities, their total lack of any

27

sense of history or suffering, their rampant consumption of useless goods
and services, and above all, their
plain dumb luck in avoiding disaster.

My own feelings are more simplistic,

> *The tragedy of the world is that the Americans*
> *are trying to run it and the British no longer do*

Bye, American readers.

Sorry, that was decidedly charmless. I didn't *really* mean it. Let us do better and agree with Albert Camus, when, in his novel 'The Fall' he told us that charm is:

A way of getting the answer yes without having asked any clear question

Welcome back Americans and let me also befriend the Jews for a while. I just love this extract from Erich Segal's 'Acts of Faith',

> *Molly was in a state of agitation, for she had just learned one of the most*
> *fundamental and least discussed rules of Jewish marriage.*
> *It was a man's <u>duty</u> to make love to his wife on Friday night –*
> *a commandment based directly on Exodus 21:10. Moreover,*
> *this obligation could not be fulfilled in a perfunctory manner,*
> *for the Law demands that he 'pleasure' her.*
> *A woman may even sue her husband if he does not.*
> *This, Deborah noted, partially explains the reason*
> *for giving husbands a hearty meal. And the smile on*
> *a Jewish woman's face when she prepares it.*

What are the requirements, other than Friday nights, for a happy life?

- *The mutual love of one person for another*
- *Good health*
- *Sufficient cash flow not to worry about paying a travel bill or making a spontaneous purchase*

- *Smiles*
- *Sunshine, for at least five hours every day*
- *Good books*
- *Good music*
- *Facility in the language of one's adopted country*
- *Good wines, readily available*
- *Quietness*
- *Solitude when necessary*
- *A few good friends*
- *To know yourself and to be yourself*
- *Not to hurt others*
- *To have the company of animals*
- *To be massaged by a beautiful girl twice a week*
- *Smart clothes*
- *A clean uncluttered mind*
- *Children and grandchildren that want to be with you*

In my 'real' home in Phuket, I have all but two of the above, but I'm working on them. How unbelievably fortunate I am.

A further requirement of mine is embodied in the wise words of John Donne, (priest, poet and preacher) written so long ago (1631) but still true today, at least for me:

To live in one land is captivite

Nevertheless, wherever we live, whatever we do, we will live longer than our allotted three score years and ten if, as well as doing the in-diet or the yoga class or breathing in the aromatherapy oils, we remember the simple advice given by William Henry Davies in his famous poem, circa 1900, entitled 'Leisure':

What is this life, if full of care,
We have no time to stand and stare?
No time to stand beneath the boughs
And stare as long as sheep or cows.
No time to see, when woods we pass,
Where squirrels hide their nuts in grass.

No time to see, in broad daylight,
Streams full of stars, like stars at night.
No time to turn at Beauty's glance
And watch her feet, how they can dance.
No time to wait till her mouth can
Enrich that smile her eyes began.
A poor life this, if full of care,
We have no time to stand and stare.

I rather bastardized another well-known verse in January 2000, sitting watching the waves sweep in and then ebb back on the beach at Nai Harn Bay; late in the afternoon, when the lobstered tourists had rushed back to their rooms for the Aloe Vera gel. It kind of describes and brings together both of the above quotations. At the time, I just had to write it down, and I really meant it then and I really mean it now, and it makes me happy, not sad:

The Sensuist

If I should die, think only this of me
That there's some corner of a golden beach
That is forever Howard.
There shall be in that rich sand
A richer soul interred,
A soul whom Asia succoured, made aware;
Gave once her roads to roam,
Her senses to enjoy;
A body of Asia's, breathing Phuket air,
Washed by the waves, blessed by tales of joy.

And think, this heart, all senses still remain,
A pulse through the eternal heart, and more.
Gives always new, the thoughts of youth compelling;
Asia's sights and sounds,
And dreams of dreams divine.
And joy, and friends and sex and gentleness;
My heart at Peace, under an Asian sun.

William Wordsworth in 1798 wrote, in his 'Lyrical Ballads'

All good poetry is the spontaneous overflow of powerful feelings.

I disagree; even bad poetry such as mine can claim the same spontaneous overflow

Let's begin to leave this chapter with a wiser man than most of us, a well-travelled man, an individual who had a genuinely individualistic way of working with and looking at other races; perhaps one might also say, a truly English way. As he said:

Everyone has a right to pronounce foreign names as he chooses

Who else but Churchill! And, I suspect he would rather agree with Sir Walter Scott when the latter proclaimed during his travels:

I begin to find that too good a character is inconvenient

Then there was the time that Belloc, travelling in Europe, met up with Chesterton and Henry James and the culture of the new and the old world turned topsy-turvy. Chesterton was sitting with Henry James when this 'person' appeared. Chesterton had believed Belloc to be in France walking with a friend, but the pair, having run out of money, had landed back in England, many days unshaven and in borrowed clothes, looking like tramps. Describing the incongruity of the scene, Chesterton many years later, wrote:

Henry James had a name for being subtle; but I think that situation was too subtle for him. I doubt to this day whether he, of all men, did not miss the irony of the best comedy in which he ever played a part. He left America because he loved Europe, and all that was meant by England or France; the gentry, the gallantry, the traditions of lineage and locality, the life that had been lived beneath the old portraits in oak-pannelled rooms. And there, on the other side of the tea-table, was Europe, was the old thing that made France and England, the posterity of the English squires and the French soldiers; ragged, unshaven, shouting for beer, shameless above all shades of poverty and wealth; sprawling, indifferent, secure. And what looked across at it was still the Puritan refinement of Boston; and the space it looked across was wider than the Atlantic

V

Can you imagine what Oscar Wilde would have to say about the long running British soap, 'Coronation Street'? – I almost wasn't quick enough to switch it off the other night when it attacked my television set. Heart stopping stuff. And as for 'Eastenders'; my goodness! What kind of world do the people that watch this terrible and tortuous claptrap inhabit? It is apparently a 'true to life' depiction, which, if it bears any reflection to reality, can only precisely describe and perpetuate everything that is wrong with the country called England. I truly cannot believe that real people actually behave like this in the privacy of their own home; that they are so unwaveringly foul and unpleasant to one another as this dreadful television programme presents. I sincerely feel that if any of my children watch either of these programmes, then they have wasted the education and opportunities we gave them. I guess I'd better not ask. However as John Mortimer in his autobiography, 'Clinging to the Wreckage' reminds us:

No one, in the whole chequered history of censorship, has ever questioned anyone's right not to read a book,
to stay away from a play or not to visit a cinema.
No one has ever suggested the compulsory sale of television sets without the button necessary to switch them off if you don't like the picture.

Thank you, Sony and the rest, for that button.

I remember the birth of television, in a true commercial sense, in England. The year was 1953 and the Queen was to be crowned.

Everyone that could afford to bought this small black and white tube, often surrounded by ostentatious wooden cabinetry and the whole family, with the neighbours who couldn't afford, sat down to watch. After a while, I have to admit, it became somewhat boring for a seven year old, so I went out to play. But these were the days of Muffin the Mule and TV decency. When the National Anthem was played at the end of transmission for the day and a quiet authoritative voice came on to remind you:

That is the end of programmes for this evening.
Please turn off your set. Goodnight everyone

How lovely.

Then, in time, decency in television programmes began to disappear and censorship had to take its place. I go along with censorship if, without it, human dignity is despoiled. GK Chesterton would have us accept that:

When people begin to ignore human dignity, it will
not be long before they begin to ignore human rights

Thinking of the world's conflicts, of man's inhumanity to man, of a world that breeds suicide bombers and irrational hatred, based on religious bigotry, Chesterton has a point.

What else is there to say about censorship? So much I guess, although living in Asia, one's mind is constantly in a state of flux, varying between it's OK to have the bar girls and the Ladyboys try to grab, admittedly always in friendship, for your exclusive jewellery, to the conviction that you don't stop at the scene of an accident to assist, just in case, as a Westerner, you might be blamed in some way for having caused it. Just because you can afford to pay. John Mortimer again,

It has been said that it is a strange anomaly of the censoring attitude that
murder is against the law, but it is no crime to write about it.
Sex is not against the law,
but to write about it has often been held a criminal offence

33

Laurie Lee, talks of his view of crime as follows. Laurie was born in Gloucestershire in 1914 and died in 1997 after completing a somehow not quite fulfilling life, never reaching the fullest potential he seemed capable of. He went to fight in the Spanish Civil War (did he know Hemingway?), but his health was not good enough to continue; then he made documentary films for the General Post Office during the Second World War. His best writing was indisputably between 1959, when he penned the autobiographical 'Cider with Rosie' and, 'As I walked out one Midsummer Morning' in 1969. He made the point that:

> *It is not crime that has increased, but its definition.*
> *The modern city, for youth, is a police trap.*
> *Our village was clearly no pagan paradise, neither were we conscious of showing tolerance. It was just the way of it. We certainly committed our share of statutory crime. Manslaughter, arson, robbery, rape, cropped up regularly throughout the years. Quiet incest flourished where the roads were bad; some found their comfort in beasts; and there were the usual friendships between men and boys who walked through the fields like lovers. Drink, animality and rustic boredom were responsible for most. The village neither approved nor disapproved, but neither did it complain to authority. Sometimes our sinners were given hell, taunted and pilloried, but their crimes were absorbed in the local scene and their punishment confined to the Parish.*

The village took care of its own; took care of the problem itself and, most importantly, never publicized what had occurred or how it had been dealt with. In this way, one can describe it as being the ultimate in community spirit; the absolute in self-care. Today, not just in the UK but in most 'developed' countries of the world, we have the 'nanny state' to *protect* us from all these 'evils', to tell us when and where we can go, when and where we can perform certain acts, even acts such as spitting, littering, smoking and pooing. Of course they are sensible, but, oh dear me....

My friend Sue, over one of her husband Michel's most wonderful margaritas, summed up the UK for me one balmy night in Phuket. She said:

As a child I could, and did, go anywhere alone. At the age of three I walked from home in Burton-on-Trent, by myself, to my kindergarten about twenty minutes away. I remember more than once, passing my Dad in the foggy morning mist as he was returning home on overnight travel from Stoke-on-Trent on the slow train; after having given a late night lecture at the Staffordshire branch of the Workers Education Association (WEA); an invention of the post war Labour Government, of which my father was a major protagonist, to provide study opportunities for people who had neither the time nor the money during their normal working day, to better themselves.

> *'Good morning, Dad', I said*
> *'Good morning, son', he replied*
> *And we went on our separate ways*

I remember when I was ten years old, that I would frequently take my tent and set it up either in our garden, open to passing strangers, or across the road in the farmer's field and sleep a blissful night away with the damp earth beneath and a starry sky above. Try letting your ten year old child do that alone now. The state would probably have you for child abuse and take your child into care. What came first, the pedophiles or the nanny state that assisted in their creation? They have always been here of course, but lacked the glorification that TV and the media have given to encourage them and their ilk. Thank goodness for a free press, many may proclaim. Although sometimes I wonder…

Childhood today, what a world for a child to grow up in! A world of terror, a world where Granddad has to prove who he is when he comes to collect you from school, despite your running happily towards his open arms and shouting at the top of your excited little voice 'Granddad!, Granddad!' – What a world!

To children, childhood holds no particular advantage

Kathleen Norris.

Kathleen was the highest paid female novelist of her time, (1880-1966), She wrote many popular romance novels that were sentimental and honest in their prose. Many of her novels are still held in high regard, although she would scarce recognise the world of today.

Let's look at happier memories of childhood; again here is charming Laurie Lee, writing in his autobiography of his childhood, spent with only females, sisters and their friends, also female. One wonders what that did to the great man.

> *On the morning of the feast Poppy Green came to the house to try on*
> *her angel's dress. She was five year's old and about my size. She had*
> *russet curls like apple peelings, a polished pumpkin face, a fruity air of*
> *exploding puddings, and a perpetual cheeky squint. I loved her, she was*
> *like a portable sweet-shop. This morning I watched my sisters dress her.*
> *She was supposed to represent a spirit. They'd made her a short frilly*
> *frock, a tinfoil helmet, cardboard wings, and a wand with a star.*
> *When they'd clothed her they stood her up on the mantelpiece and had a*
> *good look at her. Then they went off awhile on some other business and*
> *left us all alone together.*
> *'Fly!' I commanded. 'You got wings, ain't you?'*
> *Poppy squirmed and wriggled her shoulders.*
> *I grew impatient and pushed her off the mantelpiece and she fell with*
> *a howl into the fireplace. Looking down at her, smudged with coal and*
> *tears, her wand and wings all crumpled,*
> *I felt nothing but rage and astonishment.*
> *She should have been fluttering around the room.*

Wonderful! What a terrific little self-assured and honest bully he was.

However, one hopes that in later life he may have regretted his actions and listened to George Bernard Shaw when he most wisely told the world:

> *We have no more right to consume happiness without producing it*
> *than to consume wealth without producing it*

Talking of wealth, as I recall it from my childhood days; I remember taking two and sixpence every week to the Sunday School, for oh so many weeks, - so that I could go on the annual outing to Blackpool or Rhyl, - by 'luxury' coach. My sisters, Mearn and Kirsten, also took along their two and sixpences. Mum and Dad had to find that seven and six each week. At the time, I didn't realize how difficult it was for them to do that. Children can never truly appreciate how challenging it sometimes is for their parents. What they need is somehow, just there. But that's the beauty and the innocence of childhood.

But most children become parents…..unless, you subscribe to Ed Wynn's sentiment, when in 1942 he wrote:

A bachelor is a man who never made the same mistake once

Cynical. But it still doesn't remove children from the equation, Ed.

Nor do children realize, ever, how 'important' their parents are. I remember my father giving out the prizes at my (and every other school in Staffordshire) annual Speech Day. Hanley High Grammar School for Boys – and the speeches he made and my mates telling me that they hoped I'd told him not to make it a long one. I never appreciated at the time, how important he was; he was just my father. But he was also a Member of Parliament and Chairman of the Staffordshire Education Committee, responsible for all the schools, universities and colleges in Staffordshire and for their administration and budgets, *and* he was a local Councillor, (as was my mother. The phone never ever stopped ringing at home), *and* he was Chairman of the Governors of many schools, including mine, *and* he was Chairman of the Governors of Staffordshire University and of Keele University, *and* he was the main protagonist in re-building the road systems surrounding Stoke-on-Trent, including the M6 motorway *and* he was the guy that kept Shelton Iron and Steel works open for many years after the government and the steel bosses had made the decision to close it down *and* he was an advisor to Dennis Healy, then Chancellor of the Exchequer on Government fiscal policy *and*, importantly for my future development, he was a brewer of his own beer in our garage and a maker of his own jam in our undersized kitchen. All at the same bloody time! I never fully appreciated how important (and how modest) he was.

Also important at my school, admittedly some years before me, was a rather major contributor to the success of Britain in The Second World War. Reginald Mitchell. He designed the 'Spitfire', the plane that is revered for the part it played alongside the Hurricane in the dramatic 'Battle of Britain' in 1940. At the entrance to our Assembly Hall at school was one of his first propellers, made of wood! The first prototype Spitfire, flew on 5 March 1936 at Eastleigh. In later tests, it reached 349 mph and so, before the prototype had completed its official trials, the RAF ordered 310 production Spitfires. Mitchell said that 'Spitfire' was a 'Bloody silly sort of a name'.

The irony was that he never lived long enough to see the major contribution he made to keeping Britain British. I had the honour to become House Captain of Mitchell House in my final year at school.

In 1936, Mitchell was diagnosed with cancer for the second time, having defeated it once. Mitchell gave up work in early 1937, though he was often seen watching the Spitfire being tested. He went to the American Foundation in Vienna for a month, but died in June 1937. His life and the sacrifices he made to keep going despite pain and impending death were the subject of the 1942 Leslie Howard film 'The First of the Few'.

But where were we, before we wandered into my life at school? Ah, yes, we were in the realm of childhood and its relationship to parenthood. And so we come to Peter Ustinov's remembrance of his mother's attitude toward children, as recounted in his autobiography 'Dear Me,' which must surely have been significantly character forming;

The 'idea-fixe' of my mother was that it is quite natural that the cycle of love within a family should not be reciprocal, but should gravitate towards the future. In other words, she was resigned to the fact that my interest in my children should be greater than my interest in her, just as

her interest in me had been greater than her interest in her own parents.
Because of this theory of hers, she was extremely understanding and,
while very warm by nature, rather undemonstrative.

Shades of my father. But was she wrong, were either of them wrong?
I think not.

Aren't other people's children just awful. That is a rhetorical question,
thus no question mark, as there can only be one answer. It's so
unutterably dire when you visit a friend's house and they determinedly
trot out their children or their grandchildren for your delight and
approval. Even worse are the inadequate nincompoops who believe
they are achieving some form of enlightenment about themselves
through the exploration of their family lineage. All it expresses to
me is the inadequacy they feel about their own existence. Maybe Sir
Kenneth Clark in his autobiography, 'Another Part of the Wood,'
said it more succinctly, when talking of his life as a youngster in
Scotland:

> *The sight of a family tree is as distasteful to me as a VAT form.*
> *Endless bogs, not an acre of cultivated land, persistent rain,*
> *followed by swarms of midges – it did not need the villainous*
> *landlords of leftist mythology to drive people away from*
> *this melancholy, unproductive and barren coast line'*

So what is to be learned from family trees? What is there of the
slightest relevance to who we are and what we are doing today?
Because there was a felon deported to Australia or a great lover in
our lineage, does that mean that we should have a desire to go 'down
under' or to read poetry or sing songs? We have been genealogically
determined and are in possession of certain deoxyribonucleic acid
(DNA) that we inherited from our parents and maybe a little of what
our grandparents had; that's all. It's all in their genes.

Who said?

In extremis
Children can be seen,
But that is all

Ah, I remember...

And my kids didn't like it when I said it.
I have a charming daughter, Nicole, but I can't ever forget her bedroom in our apartment in Hong Kong, when, as a somewhat rebellious teenager, she was the very epitome of Ezra Pound's description of his friend, Ford Madox Ford:

I once told Fordie that if he were placed naked and alone in a room without furniture, I would come back in an hour and find total confusion

One thing I also note most strongly, (and this is where revenge for my previous statement may kick in) is,

Mothers and daughters achieve much
solace from long telephone conversations.
For fathers and sons, it is a competition.

Let's leave the last word on children with Oscar:

The young are always ready to give those who are older than themselves the full benefit of their inexperience

VI

Childhood inevitably takes on the mantle of life, what I mean is that it casts off the innocence and the honesty and joins the dishonest, corrupt and guilt of a self-seeking world. As the great pessimist, Albert Camus (if you want a fun read, grab his 'The Plague' – written sometime between his birth in 1913 and during the sadness that pervaded his life until his premature death in 1960) was prone to say:

Human life is absurd, – not because it yields no meaning, but because, yielding no meaning, human beings passionately seek one

Oh boy, – oh true!

You know, I really think it's absolute nonsense when people say that childhood and schooldays are the happiest years of your life. Poppycock. – I've never been happier than I am now, with a bit of cash in my pocket, an ability to see the world in some degree of comfort and of an age where I can tell the wankers I unfortunately meet, to go and play with themselves and leave real people alone. It's a great age!

I've been invited to the opera tonight, to hear a Korean soprano, singing in Korean. The concert lasts for two hours (not including encores!) I am reminded of what Rossini once said:

How wonderful opera would be if there were no singers!

Well, - here goes...

Back home, glass of plonk in hand; well here's my report. It's definitely an acquired taste, - the soprano, not the wine - the Koreans going wild with excitement, me listening to the warbling and screeching and hoping against hope that it would soon end, hoping also that my forced polite handclapping would not be too noticeably different from the audience's exhilaration; but I thought the piano player, sorry, concert pianist, was great. I agree with Rossini. And even more so with James Stevens, American writer and composer, who in the 1930's wrote:

Sleep is an excellent way of listening to an opera

For the two hours I was locked in my seat I couldn't help but constantly think about how many excellent bottles of wine I could have purchased for the $160 that my friend had paid for my seat. Different lives; different desires.

Talking of wine, and I promise not to go on for ever, - but it has truly been a pleasure, and continues to be one, no matter what my doctor says, - (a tip for the sixties plus fraternity, - the best cure for physical problems is to stop going to doctors), - I have made up for the time I lost as a youth.

An e-mail from my son, Russell:

Thought you and Ma would appreciate this......!!

DONT KNOW WHICH DOCTOR WROTE THIS .. BUT I LIKE HIM ... A LOT!!!

Q: I've heard that cardiovascular exercise can prolong life; is this true?

A: Your heart is only good for so many beats, and that's it... Don't waste them on exercise. Everything wears out eventually. Speeding up your heart will not make you live longer; that's like saying you can extend the life of your car by driving it faster. Want to live longer? Take a nap.

Q: Should I cut down on meat and eat more fruits and vegetables?

A: You must grasp logistical efficiencies. What does a cow eat? Hay and corn. And what are these? Vegetables. So a steak is nothing more than an efficient mechanism of delivering vegetables to your system. Need grain? Eat chicken. Beef is also a good source of field grass (green leafy vegetable). And a pork chop can give you 100% of your recommended daily allowance of vegetable products.

Q: Should I reduce my alcohol intake?

A: No, not at all. Wine is made from fruit. Brandy is distilled wine, that means they take the water out of the fruity bit so you get even more of the goodness that way. Beer is also made out of grain. Bottoms up!

Q: How can I calculate my body/fat ratio?

A: Well, if you have a body and you have fat, your ratio is one to one. If you have two bodies, your ratio is two to one, etc.

Q: What are some of the advantages of participating in a regular exercise program?

A: Can't think of a single one, sorry. My philosophy is: No Pain...Good!

Q: Aren't fried foods bad for you?

A: YOU'RE NOT LISTENING!!!. Foods are fried these days in vegetable oil. In fact, they're permeated in it. How could getting more vegetables be bad for you?

Q: Will sit-ups help prevent me from getting a little soft around the middle?

A: Definitely not! When you exercise a muscle, it gets bigger. You should only be doing sit-ups if you want a bigger stomach.

Q: Is chocolate bad for me?

A: Are you crazy? HELLO ...... Cocoa beans! Another vegetable!!! It's the best feel-good food around!

Q: Is swimming good for your figure?

A: If swimming is good for your figure, explain whales to me.

Q: Is getting in-shape important for my lifestyle?

A: Hey! 'Round' is a shape!

Well, I hope this has cleared up any misconceptions you may have had about food and diets. And remember: 'Life should NOT be a journey to the grave with the intention of arriving safely in an attractive and well preserved body, but rather to skid in sideways – Chardonnay in one hand - chocolate in the other - body thoroughly used up, totally worn out, and screaming 'WOO HOO, What a Ride!'

You know, it's as well to believe, along with Sir Walter Scott, (especially when forced to diet, - again) that:

Many of our cares are but a morbid way of looking at our privileges

Before the age of 20, I went with my sisters Mearn and Kirsten, to Savigny-en-Sancerre for a student exchange for some weeks. At the time, I didn't drink, and I was deep in the heart of the best white wine (and some not so bad red) in the world! I didn't drink alcohol until I went to Russia years later, - but that's another story I'll recount later. Anyway, in Savigny-en-Sancerre, they had, as many villages in France did at that time, horrific stories to tell of the German occupation in the Second World War. I guess I was 17 at the time, so the year would be around 1963, but they spoke of the deprivations of the war as if it were yesterday. They told us of the Germans razing the fields of produce, of taking all the potatoes of the villagers, of killing all the vines, until, finally and in shame, the villagers were forced to eat their own domestic animals and then the roaming cats and, finally, the mice and rats in the fields and in the drains. – Horrifying; reminiscent of the stories of Camus. We ate horsemeat for dinner that evening and were told it was a delicacy. For me it was stringy and only tolerably pleasant, but then I took no wine with it.

The following day I was as seriously ill as I ever remember being; violently vomiting and desperately diarrheaing. They said they would send for the doctor. I waited hours that seemed to stretch into years. Finally a black-smocked white-bearded tall figure loomed over my bed and, looking at me with sad watery eyes, began to talk in quiet lilting French; little of which I understood. But I did understand the huge gold cross around his neck and the funny shaped hat on his head and finally, I knew what it was he was doing. I was receiving the last rites! The old man was the village priest and he had kindly come to smooth my passage into the next world. That was both my scariest and my most peaceful moment in my young life hitherto. It would have been nice to die with this kind man looking at me through his tender watery eyes and his gentle smile. I could just drift away.

Then he gave me something to swallow; maybe I was taking my last communion, I was so out of it by then. I went to sleep.
Some time or some day afterwards I awoke.
'So, the doctor came and sorted you out', said my ever practical sister, Mearn. 'You can probably get up now'.
The doctor was the priest, the priest the doctor in this small town. Instead of receiving the last rites, I had been administered some medicine to calm my stomach that had been so sorely afflicted by the richness of horsemeat. In my vivid and distressed impressionable young mind I had been certain that I had eaten rats and mice and was dying of the plague.

Sometimes religion helps, sometimes it scares you stiff. Literally. As Louis Armstrong said, always a man to hedge his bets:

As far as religion, I'm a Baptist and a good friend of the Pope, and I always wear a Jewish star for luck

But my over-riding belief, especially resulting from that weird experience, goes more hand in hand with old Confucius, when he proclaimed:

What you do not want done to yourself, do not do to others

But, perhaps now is not the time to get deep into this religious thing; guilty of generating so much pain in the world, from the crusades to the fattahs. Who can really believe in any religion doing good for mankind? Maybe that's wrong, maybe the Buddhists get there, without pushing, without noise, without killing. Yes, I think they can claim the religious Nobel peace-prize, maybe the Nobel Prize for humanity in religion, if such a prize existed. Maybe there ought to be such a prize and then religions could compete for it in a true and kindly way rather than with the sword and the gun. Graham Greene had this to offer:

> *If you have abandoned one faith, do not abandon all*
> *faith. There is always an alternative to the faith we*
> *lose. Or is it the same faith under another mask?*

Taking a salutary moment's reflection leads us to a declaration by Sir Stephen Henry Roberts in the early 1950's that strikes a chord with me and, I suspect, with many others:

> *I contend that we are both atheists,*
> *I just believe in one fewer god than you do.*
> *When you understand why you dismiss all the other possible gods,*
> *you will understand why I dismiss yours*

Yet, consider the following passage from Peter Robinson, an Englishman who became a Buddhist Monk, when writing in his book, 'Phra Farang – An English Monk in Thailand':

One theme of Buddhist meditation is to contemplate corpses in various succeeding stages of decomposition and to understand, to genuinely <u>know</u> at the Insight level, that there is no escape for any of us from such a condition. Everybody accepts intellectually that the physical body will die and will be buried or burned. That intellectual acceptance of death is sometimes very shallow, though it's not entirely the point anyway. To reflect upon the impermanence and constantly changing nature of the physical body, dead or alive, can reduce our attachment to it. That

lessens the mental suffering we inflict upon ourselves when the body
becomes sick, old, no longer handsome or beautiful, or starts to let us
down in various ways. That penetrative understanding can then help
us to understand the impermanence of all other phenomena as well. It is
our attachment and clinging to impermanent phenomena which is the
main cause of our mental suffering. Impermanent phenomena means
everything, since there are no phenomena with any permanence.
With that Insight understanding about impermanence, we can change
the way we view not only our own body, but also our reactions
to other people, things, situations and everything around us.

Take a moment to read that again, it's worth it.

Consider this statement for a moment, from Albert Camus, writing in his novel, 'The Plague':

God did not exist, since otherwise there would be no need for priests

But let's take a priest and explore, with GK Chesterton, at least for a moment, what the value is of such an office:

When a Catholic comes from confession he does truly, by definition,
step out again into the dawn of his own beginning and look with
new eyes across the world to a Crystal Palace that is really of crystal.
He believes that in that dim corner, and in that brief ritual, God
has really re-made him in His own image. He is now a new
experiment of the Creator. He is as much a new experiment as he
was when he was really five years old. He stands, as I have said,
in the white light at the worthy beginning of the life of a man.
He may be grey and gouty; but he is only five minutes old.

What a great priest and a great religion to make you believe that!

A salutary thought to challenge the traditions of real believers may come from thinkers such as James Ward, when he tests us with the thought:

What would Jupiter be without a beard?
Who would countenance a shaved Christ?

How deep is faith? How dependant upon trappings?

The oddest of people pontificate, sometimes wisely and well, about odd faiths; here is the ex-heavyweight boxing champion of the world's dad, The Reverend George Edward Foreman, speaking as part of a simplistic sermon he preached in 1990, telling us:

Some people don't even believe in a supernatural God. I wouldn't serve
a god who wouldn't speak to me. I was talkin' to a fella one time and he
told me he turned toward somewhere and prayed eight or nine times a
day. And he showed me how he put his head down to the ground. I said,
'Man, does God ever speak to you?' He said, 'No.'
I said, 'Hey, brother, ain't nobody home.'

The 'ain't nobody home' has worked well for atheists (of which I am one) and sometimes agnostics for many years. But it is the 'sometimes' for agnostics that doesn't sit well with me, or indeed with the guy who wrote the following, who, for the moment, I can't honestly remember. I think it might have been Yann Martel in 'The Life of Pi' – it sounds like him. I'll try to discover who it was exactly by the time I put this book to bed. Anyway, whoever it was, said it apropos agnostics:

It is not atheists who get stuck in my craw, but agnostics.
Doubt is useful for a while.
We must all pass through the garden of Gethsemane.
If Christ played with doubt, so must we.
If Christ spent an anguished night in prayer, if He burst out
from the Cross, 'My God, my God, why have you forsaken
me?' Then surely we are also permitted doubt. But we must
move on. To choose doubt as a philosophy of life is akin to
choosing immobility as a means of transportation

Is there any hope for any faith? Why not just choose one for mankind? But then it will be argued, it has to be the *right* one....

48

There is no faith that has never yet been broken,
except that of a truly faithful dog

So said Konrad Lorenz

Dog faith? Faith in dogs? Is that the new religion that could save mankind?
Mind you, Rita Rudner may have a point when she asks:

I wonder if other dogs think poodles are members of a weird religious cult.

The Dalai Lama believes that;

Love and compassion are the essence of all religion

Were, - Dali Lama, - were

VII

Can you imagine life without music and books? Any and all music. Any and all books. Well, I'm not too convinced about Chinese Opera, but almost all else. I remember appreciating my first classical piece, which was Beethoven's Violin Concerto in D, which I played almost daily in my small student room on campus at Keele University; when I was studying English and Sociology as mains and Astronomy, Psychology and Historical Theology as subsids. I only lasted there for one year before I was requested to leave. I wish I could give you a juicy sex scandal that caused my hasty departure from the hallowed halls and pathways, but the truth was far less sublime. However, I had in that time discovered Beethoven and TS Eliot; how to fence with a sword, actually a rapier; developed an understanding of egotistical hedonism, a dictum advising that we always put ourselves first for self-gratification, no matter what we do; even including where we may be called upon to save the lives of others and how and why we always feel immediate pleasure and relief at hearing of the death of someone we know, pleasure and relief, at a subconscious level, because we are the one that has survived. And I learned how to talk knowingly about onomatopoeia, and even to spell it! Mind you, Peter Ustinov, never a great advocate of accurate spellmanship; a fact which astonishes and bewilders me, was perhaps correct in stating in his autobiography, 'Dear Me':

The insistence on accurate spelling at modern schools is an effort to invest a living language with rigor mortis, and to prepare a rhapsodic means of self-expression for the glacial corridors of computerdom

I am also rather fond of Frank Lloyd Wright's statement as the 20th Century blossomed:

> *I'm all in favour of keeping dangerous weapons out of the hands of fools. Let's start with typewriters*

We are to meet fools a-plenty later on.

Anyway, for the moment, back to music:

Oscar, always present, always with the right words:

> *I can fancy a man who had led a perfectly commonplace life, hearing by chance some curious piece of music, and suddenly discovering that his soul, without his being conscious of it, had passed through terrible experiences, and known fearful joys, or wild romantic loves, or great renunciations.*

I'm watching a DVD as I write this. It is John Denver, quietly and modestly explaining how he came to write some of his most wonderful songs, like Rocky Mountain High and Calypso (just listen again to the lyrics, no, that demeans them, to the poetry of the words and to the sentence composition of this greatest of great songs and I challenge you not to be moved, even to tears.) Then, a little known song of his insinuates itself into this video – a song he wrote while the first unsuccessful (in that it didn't finish the job and remove Saddam the first time, thereby allowing all the terror, heartbreak and bloodshed that occurred when again we were unsuccessful in completing the job) Gulf War was at its peak and a soldier writes home wishing his sweetheart was with him, not in the war, but just with him wherever he was, in Iraq, in Paris, in London. The song is called, 'Wish you were here' and if you have ever loved anyone and if you can watch John Denver performing this song on the video without a huge lump in your throat or tears spilling, then please throw away this little book of mine for you and I do not have a meeting of the minds.

Ulysses S. Grant, 18th President of the USA must have been a very sad man indeed, as he was often heard to pronounce:

I know only two tunes, one is Yankee Doodle, the other isn't

Maybe he and the Zangiacomo band from Joseph Conrad's novel 'Victory' have much in common

The Zangiacomo band was not making music; it was simply murdering silence with a vulgar, ferocious energy. One felt as if witnessing a deed of violence; and that impression was so strong that it seemed marvellous to see the people sitting so quietly on their chairs, drinking so calmly out of their glasses, and giving no signs of distress, anger, or fear.

Moving from music, we may return later; let us allow Oscar to lead us in a short study of some books:

The books that the world calls immoral are books that show the world its shame

Do you remember the nonsense of Mary Whitehouse and other anal retentives complaining about the immorality of those wonderful books, 'Sons and Lovers'; 'Lady Chatterley's Lover' and 'Women in Love', penned by that extraordinarily gifted writer, DH Lawrence? This is what he had to say at the time:

The censor-moron does not really hate anything but the living and growing human consciousness

This little book of mine is composed of quotes, some quirky, some clever, but when I re-read 'Women in Love' some years ago, I simply wrote in my book of quotations that 'Almost ALL of Women in Love' deserved to be in my book of quotations. The writing is so keen, so wonderful, so evocative, so realistic, so bloody good!

But then suddenly, we can be surprised with excellent and evocative descriptive writing from, perhaps, the most unlikely of sources. Here is John Grisham with an outstanding piece of descriptive writing from his novel, 'The Last Juror', - who would think to study Grisham in this way? To set the scene all you need to know is that the newspaper has gone into liquidation:

When the crying stopped, he suddenly stood, bit his lip, and announced,
   'I've got to tell mother (that he, the owner/editor has to sell the
   paper she still partly owned) *The three of us looked at each other.*
Miss Emma Caudle had departed this life years earlier, but her feeble
   heart continued to work just barely enough to postpone a funeral. She
   neither knew nor cared what color Jell-O they were feeding her, and
   she certainly cared nothing about Ford County and its newspaper.
   She was blind and deaf and weighed less than eighty pounds, and
   now Spot was about to discuss involuntary bankruptcy with her.
   At this point, I realized that he, too, was no longer with us.

Even simpler and perhaps more vivid, comes this wonderfully evocative sentence in Laura Hillenbrand's charming book, 'Seabiscuit':

He had a colourless translucence about him that made him seem
   as if he were in the earliest stages of progressive invisibility.

Now compare these extracts with the (I've heard it said) appalling writing, in a descriptive sense, from another modern and popular novelist, Colin Forbes, (who has penned more than thirty, many say, trite 'blockbusters'), stringing the following words together (from his novel, 'No Mercy', - I wish he'd given us some):

'We'll wait here awhile,' Tweed explained after a few minutes. 'Just in
   case whoever is responsible organized a back-up ambush for us nearer
   London. They'll think we've turned off to Guildford or somewhere else.'
He paused to taste the coffee. 'This is very good.' 'So is this,' said Paula,
   who had sampled her cake. 'The cream's very fresh. Where are we now
   with this horrific case? It's good to get away from Dartmoor.
   At Abbey Grange I wondered where Drago Volkanian was.'
   'One of the things I hope to discover from Lucinda.
   You've had a rough ride, so take your time.'
   Eventually they left the café and the sun came out, casting
   a cheerful light over fields where sheep grazed.

Ugh!...

As Ambrose Bierce wrote at the end of the 19ᵗʰ Century:

The covers of this book are too far apart

How prophetic and he hadn't even read it!

So why do people buy this guy's novels, certainly not for the ability of the writer to write evocative passages, but rather, I suppose, to grip the reader with a story line, as does an action movie. Who ever listens to the dialogue in an action movie? It's totally incidental. So with Forbes's novels, the words he writes and his craftsmanship, or lack of, is incidental to the plot and its vagaries. Good for him, especially if you want to be remembered for making money rather than the ability to write. Remember old Charlie Dickens, - greatest writer of his era, rarely a penny in his pocket, so too with Oscar and with Dylan Thomas and with DH Lawrence and on and on and on... Stanley Matthews hardly made any money out of football and he was the greatest of them all; both on and off the pitch. Look what the world gives to the trumped up youngsters of today, who can kick a ball just about as well as they can express themselves in words of more than one syllable. Oh, the world has gone mad! – Or perhaps it's me and I should be listening to the wisdom of Bernard Shaw:

The moment we want to believe something, we suddenly see all the arguments for it, and become blind to the arguments against it

Or even, from the always correct Benjamin Disraeli, the first and thus far, the only person of Jewish parentage to serve (twice) as Prime Minister of The UK who would have us realize that:

It is much easier to be critical than to be correct

And Calvin Coolidge would add:

Doubters do not achieve,
Skeptics do not contribute,
Cynics do not create

I have added a number of quotations to this little book that I don't personally subscribe to, - just for you to know.

Let's see if Churchill can add a thought or two, admittedly in a wildly different context, but after all, we can play around with contexts, can't we?

We know that he (Churchill was actually talking about
Ramsey MacDonald but, hey ho) *has, more than any
other man, the gift of compressing the largest amount
of words into the smallest amount of thought*

For once, the same thought was expressed even better than by Churchill's erudition when Christopher Morley declared:

*The unluckiest insolvent in the world is the man whose
expenditure of speech is too great for his income of ideas*

However, balancing my diatribe could be Tom Stoppard who, in his 'Artist Descending a Staircase' gave Colin Forbes all the support he requires:

*Unprovided with original learning, unformed in the habits of thinking,
unskilled in the arts of composition, I resolved to write a book.*

But I still rather adhere to the view of Edward Gibbon, who luckily (living from 1737 to 1794 – another guy that didn't make it to 60!) had no opportunity to read the work of Colin Forbes or members of his equally gifted ilk:

*Your manuscript is both good and original, but the part that is
good is not original and the part that is original is not good.*

And so enters the ever erudite and ever exact Oscar when he advises:

There is no such thing as a moral or an immoral book.
Books are well written or badly written. That is all.

But, he was also pretty smart and saved himself a lot of agro by declaring:

I am too fond of reading books to care to write them

Do yourself a real favour, even if you don't finish my little book of rambles, - get yourself to a bookshop and buy 'Birdsong' by Sebastian Faulks, a magnificent and deeply moving novel, ISBN 0-09-938791-3, published in 1994 by Vintage. It's a pity that Oscar died too long ago to have the pleasure of reading something of this elegance and poignancy. And from a man born in 1953, some 35 years after the scenes he depicts with great detail and insightfulness. As 'Art & Culture' describe Mr. Faulks and his writing:

Love and war may be huge themes, but Sebastian Faulks approaches
them from a microscopic perspective. He detects love in the minute
movements of a woman's fingers; in a man's manner of crawling
through trenches, he captures fear and torment. Faulks is involved
in a romance with detail, charging every object and every gesture
with emotion and significance. In his hands, description ceases to be
topical or comprehensive and becomes physical and intuitive. Like
Balzac and Flaubert, he is an adept at the art of selecting those
salient features of reality in which emotions are concentrated

Let us linger for a lighter moment over the delightfully descriptive, almost redolent prose of James Elliott in his memoirs 'All Things Wise and Wonderful'

It (the war) vanished as the wide sweep of grey-blue sea fell beneath
the rising ground behind the town, and as the bus trundled westward
I looked out on a landscape of untroubled peace. The long moist
furrows of the new-turned soil glittered under the pale February sun,

contrasting with the gold stubble fields and the grassy pastures where sheep clustered around their feeding troughs. There was no wind and the smoke rose straight from the farm chimneys and the bare branches of the roadside trees were still as they stretched across the cold sky'

Just delightful, but somewhat removed from the linguistic competence of many novelists of today. Let's take another and see if she can write.

Is the novel, 'Trace' by Patricia Cornwell, a contemporary of Forbes, well or badly written? If it keeps us turning the pages, maybe it's well-written. Is the following extract well-written?

The detective, his name's Browning, seems all right but he's not been doing homicides long and the cases he has worked are of the urban renewal variety. One piece of shit shooting another piece of shit'

I personally think it's brilliant; you can see the man (Detective Marino), you can hear his gratingly unsubtle voice and you can really believe he said exactly this and, wow, from where did she drag that image of 'urban renewal'; classically original!

Compare again with what went before:

He paused to taste the coffee. 'This is very good.' 'So is this,'said Paula, who had sampled her cake. 'The cream's very fresh. Where are we now with this horrific case? It's good to get away from Dartmoor. At Abbey Grange I wondered where Drago Volkanian was.' 'One of the things I hope to discover from Lucinda. You've had a rough ride, so take your time.'

Say no more...

Thank goodness that Patricia did not heed the advice from the pulpit in a sermon preached by J.W. Burgon in 1871:

When, instead of rejoicing in the retirement of her home and the strict
privacy of her domestic duties, she is found to be secretly longing for
the publicity of print and the notoriety of the platform; when this,
or any approach to this, becomes a common thing, - woman will too
late discover that she has, as far as in her lay, unsexed herself; lost
her present unique social position; come to be regarded only as an
inferior kind of man. Man, with all his hardness: man without his
manliness. She will no longer be a help and consolation. She will
inevitably find that she has dethroned herself, - to her own heavy
harm and loss; to our abiding sorrow and increasing discomfort.

Although we may wish that scores of other women had done just
that!

There really is no excuse for lethargy in excellence as regards the
written word and phrase. How is it that a man born of Polish parents
in the Russian dominated Ukraine, who became a simple seaman,
rising to the position of master mariner, could with dint of study
and applied passion, come to write, in the English language, utterly
eruditely and supremely well? A language he was not exposed to until
the age of 21! Come on, Colin, try a little harder. Open any page of
any novel by Joseph Conrad (Josef Teodor Konrad Korzeniowski)
and you will discover linguistic excellence:

An unsuspected stream of loquacity had broken its dam somewhere
deep within the man, had diluted his fiery blood and softened
his pitiless fibre. Schomberg experienced mingled relief and
apprehension, as if suddenly an enormous savage cat had begun
to wind itself about his legs in inexplicable friendliness.

(this from 'Victory' – but, as I say, open any page of any of Conrad's
supremely well-written novels and give yourself a linguistic treat.
Take it with a bottle of your favourite wine. Your very best wine;
nothing else will be good enough to compliment the experience you
are about to encounter.)

Go on, if he can do it, at least we can all 'try harder'.

Off this tack (very seamanlike!) and onto windward. Let us consider true farce for a moment; does it hold the mirror up to anything? Is it something that we enjoy? Do we think of farce as comedy? I think that we'd better understand something, from the undisputed master of farce, the great and sometimes little appreciated actor, Brian Rix, who, writing in his autobiography in 1977, 'My farce from my elbow', penned:

> The whole point of a good farce is that it teeters on the edge of tragedy. It always threatens ultimate catastrophe, and this is what sustains the dramatic tension. But by a slight twist it makes people roll about with laughter. It is tragedy with its trousers down.

He is far too modest, he is far too simple, he is far too astute for most of us to appreciate what he is really telling us. Rock on Brian!

But those of us who dabble with the written word, who believe we may just be poised to give the world the 'Great Novel', would do well to enjoy a salutary thought from a master, such as Ernest Hemingway, when he advised:

> There is no use writing anything that has been written before unless you can beat it. What a writer in our time has to do is write what hasn't been written before or beat dead men at what they have done.

Let us recover our psyche and dwell for a moment with a modest sliver of gifted insight, as we soak up this piece from DH Lawrence and recognise how well words, in the hands of a definitive craftsman, can be structured to complete a sound idea. Savouring any of Lawrence's writing transports us to another space, a liberty of the mind. The quotation is from 'Women in Love':

> I don't believe in love at all – that is, any more than I believe in hate, or in grief. Love is one of the emotions like all the others – and so it is all right whilst you feel it. But I can't see how it becomes an absolute. It is just part of human relationships, no more. And it is only part of any human relationship. And why one should be required always to feel it, any more than one always feels sorrow

59

or distant joy, I cannot conceive. Love isn't a desideratum – it is an emotion you feel or you don't feel, according to circumstance.'

(In case you're not familiar with the word 'desideratum', it means a thing lacked and wanted, a requirement.)

Reading Lawrence makes us recall the famous quotation from Francoise Sagan who at the age of 43 in 1979 reminded us of what many of us feel:

> *The only thing I regret is that I will never have time to read all the books I want to read*

Although, if he were to take the advice of Lady Astor, (not Churchill's greatest admirer or friend, by the way), he may have the time. She said:

> *I refuse to admit that I'm more than fifty-two. Even if that does make my sons illegitimate.*

However, why not regard good and great books in a different light, as animate objects of love and friendship; William Feather had this to say:

> *Finishing a good book is like leaving a good friend*

I have left so many good friends in my life; but have decided that when I slow down, put my feet up in my lounger around my pool in the tropics with a glass in my hand, I will re-make their acquaintance. I will hope to emulate the words of Franz Kafka and remain youthful, at least in thought if not in body:

> *Anyone who keeps the ability to see beauty never grows old*

VIII

Why?

Lord Byron	36
Peter Sellers	55
Tony Hancock	44
John Denver	54
James Dean	24
John Lennon	40
JFK	46
Billy Fury	43
Oscar Wilde	46
Christopher Reeve	52
Will Shakespeare	52
Buddy Holly	23
DH Lawrence	45
Elvis	42 who announced (when admittedly, he was quite young in the business,)

I don't know anything about music. In my line you don't have to

Charles Dickens	58
Eric Morecambe	58
Martin Luther King	39 who said, shortly before he was assassinated:

In the end, we will remember not the words of our enemies, but the silence of our friends

Robbie Burns	37
Mozart	35

Steve Irwin	44
Richard Burton	59
Dylan Thomas	39
Jesus Christ	33

All before sixty!

And then why?

Gadaffi	64+
Yassar Arafat	75
Castro	80+
General De Gaulle	90
Idi Amin	78
Pinochet	90+
Sadaam Hussein	69+
Mao	83
Stalin	74
Ferdinand Marcos	72
Benito Mussolini	62
Pol Pot	73
Ayatollah Khomeini	88

Only the good die young

But thank goodness for the over 60's that just keep (kept) on going:

Paul Anka
Sir John Mills
Richard Branson
Winston Churchill
PG Wodehouse, who at the age of 93, told us of his lifestyle:

I get up awfully early, have my breakfast about quarter past eight, and then generally work after breakfast. When I've got any work to do, when I'm doing a novel, I always give up the morning to it. And then, after lunch, Ethel and I go out to pick up the mail, take the two dogs down to the water, run them around, and get back here about five-o-clock. After that I just read.

A great deal more activity than many a 40 year old!

Muhammad Ali
Jimmy Carter
Mother Teresa
Elton John
Dirk Bogarde
Bill Clinton, - who now, most thankfully, is respected and regarded for what he has done and is doing so well; but still cannot quite get away from the mire that, perhaps, was best described by the comedian actor Robin Williams, when, discussing the Lewinsky episode when he reminded us that:

> *God gave men both a penis and a brain, but unfortunately not enough blood supply to run both at the same time*

But thank God, he also gave us Clinton

Sinatra
Donald Sutherland
Larry King
Sir Alec Guinness
Queen Elizabeth ll
Al Pacino
Paul MaCartney
Kirk Douglas
Olivier
Alistair Cooke
And…. dear, ever youthful and mysterious, - Cliff, who will probably NEVER get old enough to enjoy the final sport as described by Lord Grey of Falloden in 1927 when he advised us that:

> *I am getting to an age when I can only enjoy the last sport left. It is called hunting for your spectacles*

But let me give the last word of this section to that great and glorious, although heartbreaking, world-renowned comedian Benny Hill, who simply said:

I don't believe that I'll never see your skies or your trees again,
The women were fine, and so was the wine,
And I shouldn't complain; but then,
You give such damn short rides in this fairground of yours, Lord,
Please may I go round again?

Benny, worth around £10 million, died alone, aged 68, in April 1992. His body remained undiscovered for days in his tiny suburban house.

IX

Let's talk about sex for a while, it's the greatest, the strongest animal and human (humans are animals of course, - actually, some of the worst of the animal species, especially as far as cruelty and garbage are concerned) drive. Stronger even than the drive for food or nurture. Often stronger than the drive for survival. But maybe sex, as in procreation, is in itself, survival. Have you ever seen a hungry male lion still trying to get it up a lioness in heat, instead of searching the veldt for food? I have.

I am reminded of Richard Burton, greatest of actors, saddest of losses, pontificating, as he loved to do in his natural deep Welsh brogue:

'Having discovered sex,
I began looting and plundering it with great delight.'

Personally, I was a late developer as far as sexual prowess was concerned. But then I grew up in the sixties when the press, everywhere, was reporting the wave of free love and flower power sweeping the land. What an invention! It never swept anywhere near where I was. Perhaps I was somewhat foolishly too committed to one girl or maybe Stoke-on-Trent was the only city in the UK in the sixties that the flower power people and the drug pushers avoided. It certainly feels like it in retrospect. Maybe when they reached as far north as Stafford, they decided to carry straight on up the new motorway to the Lake District where they could flop around with Wordsworth's daffodils, making all the free love that this poetically weird and wonderful part of England could endure. Anyway, they missed me. Even I sadly believe, they missed the university (Keele, North Staffordshire) where I was ensconced for a year (only a year) in 1965. Can you believe it? It's true. I remember how boringly chaste we all were and trying to, but frequently failing in our duty to lay and get laid. Instead, we would be discovering, analysing and reading together the works of TS Eliot and Plato. Honestly! Bloody hell!

I shudder to think what my children were able to do when their turn came around. I honestly don't believe promiscuity was rife in the sixties. If was a fringe affair and the newspapers sold stories pretending the fringe was the mainstream. Hell, people still went to church on a Sunday in the sixties and went to their girlfriend's home for Sunday tea and didn't say 'fuck' half as much as they do today, and never ever in films or on TV or in books. – The sixties for me was a sweet and innocent time and I look back on it with a warmness and joy of discovery that I have rarely felt since.

X

Let's now go on a little journey through the decades

What would a person born in 1946 have experienced by the time he or she reached 60? I was born in September 1946, one year after the end of the Second World War:

The war to end all wars

Don't you just wish! That war claimed almost 60 million lives and still we're at it!

Other than my birth and that of Timothy Dalton (007 - very briefly), Jack Straw and Robin Cooke (politicians of some note), George Best, (arguably the best British footballer ever, save for Stanley Mathews) and Paul McCartney, (arguably the best song writer and performer ever), the year was most notable for being the year in which the bikini was invented. How do you 'invent' a bikini? It's like saying you invented a pair of trousers or a skirt. It already existed for countless Aeons; the simple truth was that the World War had so liberated women that they could now wear it in public without other coverings, and on beaches and in fashion parades. But have you ever seen some of the bikinis of the 1940's? Hardly sexy; although, if I had been 20 years old and just back from the continent where I had been living in a mud trench and not seen a woman for a couple of years, it might have had me frothing at the mouth.

Personally, I rather like the description penned by Joey Adams;

A bikini is like a barbed-wire fence.
It protects the property without obstructing the view

However, Aaron Levenstein may have been a little more erudite in his description:

Statistics are like a bikini. What they reveal is
suggestive, but what they conceal is vital

The 20th century, the century of my birth and, I guess, most of my life, is depicted by the on-line encyclopedia as:

A century that witnessed radical changes in almost every area
of human activity. Accelerating scientific understanding, better
communications and faster transportation transformed the world
in those hundred years more than any time in the past. It was a
century that started with steam-powered ships and ended with
the space shuttle. Horses and other pack animals, Western society's
basic form of personal transportation for thousands of years, were
replaced by automobiles within the span of a few decades.

But that statement somehow doesn't capture the essence of the years from 1940 to 2000. Many were the years of hope, of:

Let's be frank about it; most of our people have never had it so good

So said Harold Macmillan – affectionately known, at least in the early years of his Prime Ministership, as 'Supermac'

Of:

The wind of change is blowing through the continent. Whether we like
it or not, this growth of national consciousness is a political fact....

Again, this from 'Supermac'

Of:

We are more popular than Jesus now

Naughty of you, John, but you did apologise later, - didn't you? (August 11 - The Beatles hold a press conference in Chicago, during which John Lennon apologizes for his 'more popular than Jesus' remark, saying, 'I didn't mean it as a lousy anti-religious thing.') Some apology that was John.

Of:

*We all remember where we were when we heard the
news of the assassination of John Kennedy*

I was 17 years old at the time and I haven't the foggiest idea where I was or what I was doing when I heard the news. I guess it just wasn't important enough to me. But I do remember where and what I was doing when I heard that Elvis had died. Whose death made most impact on you in your formative years? Who was it that, like Elvis, couldn't possibly have died, for everyone was immortal in our seminal years, weren't they? Was Elvis as dumb as some historians would have us believe?

Ambition is a dream with a V8 engine

Said he. Wisely?

*Don't criticize what you don't understand, son.
You never walked in that man's shoes.*

Even more wisely?

*I have no use for bodyguards, but I have a very special use
for two highly trained certified public accountants*

Sublimely wise?

As Paul Anka penned and millions have sung over the years, expressing their 20th Century wish, and sometimes the reality of a life they, like Sinatra, spent:

And now the end is near
And so I face the final curtain,
My friends, I'll say it clear,
I'll state my case of which I'm certain.
I've lived a life that's full, I've travelled each and evr'y highway
And more, much more than this, I did it my way.

Only a year ago I saw Paul Anka on stage in Seoul. He was outstanding; he must be near 70 years old and was singing, dancing and captivating an audience composed largely of people one third of his age. Tremendous vitality and showmanship.

Have you done it 'your way', or someone else's way? I think, for most of us it has been and continues to be a compromise and maybe compromise is, after all, 'My Way'.

Or is that a cop out?

As we get older, perhaps we should agree with Somerset Maugham:

Dying is a very dull, dreary affair. And my advice to
you is to have nothing whatever to do with it

After decades of fight of the women's suffrage movement, the right to vote for women was introduced in all western countries by the 1960's, prompting many anti-male movements. Even in literature, even in little books like mine:

If you have any doubts that we live in a society controlled
by men, try reading down the index of contributors to a
volume of quotations, looking for women's names.

Proclaimed Elaine Gill. Guilty as charged, but then we must ask ourselves, why?

Communism became a major force in global politics, especially after the Second World War, spreading its insidious disease all over the globe: most notably in Eastern Europe, China, Indochina and Cuba. This led to the Cold War and proxy wars with the West, including wars in Korea (1950-1953) and Vietnam (1957-1975). I don't think that Henrich Heine, German poet and writer in the early 1800's was far from the mark when he wrote:

Communism possesses a language which every people can understand – its elements are hunger, envy, and death

Conversely, the same period also saw the end of colonialism, which led to the independence of many African and Asian countries. The creation of Israel, a Jewish state in a mostly Arab region of the world, fueled many conflicts in the region, which were also influenced by the vast oil fields in many of the Arab countries.

A conquered nation is like a man with cancer, he can think of nothing else

Offered the shrewd George Bernard Shaw. And now that cancer has been turned on the colonisers. Fair play? We should have listened to Mark Twain:

It is easier to stay out than get out

Are you listening, Bush, Blair, et al?

When the century began, Paris was the artistic capital of the world, where both French and foreign writers, composers and visual artists gathered. By the end of the century, the focal point of culture had moved to the United States, especially New York City and Los Angeles and it became subject to Alvin Toffler's (American Sci-fi author) 'Law of Raspberry Jam':

The wider any culture is spread, the thinner it gets

Lord Raglan was just a little kinder when he shared his thoughts on culture with us:

Culture is roughly anything we do and the monkeys don't

I think that what we mean by culture went through a fundamental metamorphosis once the centre crossed the Atlantic, I'm not saying better or worse, just very very different. Our standards altered, our definitions were redefined and our acceptance of what could be included in culture went through a dramatic transition, one that would readily embrace Lord Raglan's description.

Rock and Roll and Jazz styles of music were, at this time, becoming all the rage in the United States and quickly became the dominant forms of popular music in America and later in the rest of the world. What occurred in the deep South, transferred northwards, was re-defined and refined in the cellars of Liverpool, from whence it was exported back to America and thence throughout the world; even being listened to clandestinely in Red China and in the then repressive Soviet Union.

In the year of mine and Paul's and Robin's and George's birth, Winston Churchill invented 'The Iron Curtain'. The speech in which he coined this phrase may be regarded as the most important that Churchill delivered as Leader of the Opposition (1945-1951). It contained certain phrases – 'the special relationship,' 'the sinews of peace' - which at once entered into general use and have survived. But it is the passage on 'the iron curtain' that attracted immediate international attention and had incalculable impact upon public opinion in the United States and in Western Europe. Russian historians date the beginning of the Cold War from this speech; Churchill said:

From Stettin in the Baltic to Trieste in the Adriatic, an iron curtain has descended across the Continent. Behind that line lie all the capitals of the ancient states of Central and Eastern Europe. Warsaw, Berlin, Prague, Vienna, Budapest, Belgrade, Bucharest and Sofia, all these famous cities and the populations around them lie in what I must call the Soviet sphere, and all are subject in one

*form or another, not only to Soviet influence but to a very high
and, in many cases, increasing measure of control from Moscow.*

While the curtain came down, fortunately sports became an important part of society, bringing nations closer together and becoming an activity not only for the privileged. Watching sports, later also on television, became a popular activity, although Lee Loevinger was a little unkind (wasn't he?) when he declared:

> *Television is the literature of the illiterate, the culture of
> the low-brow, the wealth of the poor, the privilege of the
> underprivileged, the exclusive club of the excluded masses*

I do feel this quite often; especially when I switch on to find interminable repeats of second class comedy and soaps constantly recurring on the channel the BBC now euphemistically calls the 'Entertainment' Channel. It is about as entertaining as watching the proverbial drying of paint. But I suspect that Loevinger has probably never watched the Animal Channel or The Discovery Channel. Maybe his opinion might change?

As our 20th Century progressed, antibiotics drastically reduced mortality from bacterial diseases and their prevalence and a vaccine was developed for polio, ending a worldwide epidemic. I remember a lad my own age dying of polio in my first year at Hanley High Grammar School for Boys. It was a stunningly dramatic event in our early school life and for weeks afterwards, we all went around watching each other for signs and symptoms that might mean that we too had caught the deadly disease. It was an uneasy first year at that school.

X-rays became a powerful diagnostic tool for a wide spectrum of diseases, from bone fractures to cancer. The development of vitamins virtually eliminated scurvy and other vitamin-deficiency diseases. I recollect being told by my grandparents and uncles of the numbers of people they had experienced in their lives, especially in the time of war, who had suffered and died from malnutrition and scurvy. And I am only 60 years old. How the world has moved along, - at least the Western World and most of Asia. But Africa, the Sudan?

Contraceptive drugs were developed. I remember the pill coming out and wondering which of the girls I knew were secretly sinking the little white saviour as they put their head on the pillow. Just think what relief from emotional distress that little white tablet instantly offered humanity, as well as of course, assisting the more politically correct reduction in world population growth rates.

Choose the quotation you like best, there are hundreds on this much loved and much abused subject:

The best contraceptive for old people is nudity

So said Phyllis Diller and, with her body, she was the absolute living proof. In the same vein:

My best birth control now is just to leave the lights on

Suggested Joan Rivers; whereas Margaret Smith recommends an original remedy:

The best contraceptive is the word 'no'- repeated frequently

Gosh, who would have thought of that? Margaret was obviously lacking in tact, and fun. Woody Allen can be counted upon to bring a little more realism into the topic:

I want to tell you a terrific story about oral contraception.
I asked this girl to sleep with me and she said 'No.'

But in my (somewhat extensive − 4 children, 5 grandchildren) experience, Carole Tabron has it right:

A crying baby is the best form of birth control

AIDS killed millions of people in the 20th Century and continues to wreak havoc today. It's something that simply didn't exist for me, at least as far as public knowledge and concern was involved, until well after I was married and had kids of my own. AIDS treatments still remain inaccessible to people living with HIV/AIDS in developing countries, but even with the best available treatment, most patients eventually die from AIDS, even now, even today.

However, in counterpoint, because of increased life span, the prevalence of old age diseases, including Alzheimer's disease and Parkinson's disease has dramatically increased and the world waits for the researchers in proteins, in cell signalling and in DNA research to come up with a method, probably by means of a protein chip, to diagnose the likely occurrence of these diseases and to suggest what might be done to minimise or at least delay their effects. The world waits, but as the American journalist, Andy Rooney, points out:

Because over the past few years, more money has been spent on breast implants and Viagra than is spent on Alzheimer's Disease research, it is believed that by the year 2030 there will be a large number of people wandering around with huge breasts an...

Read it again if you didn't get it first time.

Do you remember using your first Polaroid camera (invented in 1947)? What a thrill to be able to create a picture actually in your own hands and to have it available within a minute! The pictures did tend to fade a bit so, when you finally convinced her to stand provocatively there in the nude, your time sensitive clock was already ticking. But for me, the Baby Brownie 127 was the best. One colour of casing (black of course), a little red button for the click and a manual wind on and on and on. It was one of my earliest and most supreme possessions and I guarded my Brownie with my life.

From Patrick Dempsey:

The box brownie was the camera 120 film was introduced with... way back 106 years ago!!! Great shots! Once again proving that all

the hype about elements and multicoatings is just that... hype! You can
get great images out of these old wooden and cardboard cameras!

In the year 1949 two events occurred almost simultaneously that were to have a tremendous effect upon the world and its thinking. One, almost certainly, as a direct circumstance of the other. China became Communist and George Orwell published his influential novel, 'Nineteen Eighty-Four':

Communism is the death of the soul. It is the organisation
of total conformity – in short, of tyranny, - and it
is committed to making tyranny universal

So said Adlai Stevenson, the US Ambassador to the United Nations from 1961 to 1965, whilst George Orwell was writing:

Book One, Chapter 1 of '1984':

Winston had disliked her from the very first moment of seeing her.
He knew the reason. It was because of the atmosphere of hockey-
fields and cold baths and community hikes and general clean-
mindedness which she managed to carry about her. He disliked
nearly all woman, and especially the young and pretty ones, who
were the most bigoted adherents of the party, the swallowers of
slogans, the amateur spies and nosers-out of unorthodoxy.

The thought police would get him just the same. He had
committed—would have committed, even if he had never set pen
to paper—the essential crime that contained all others in itself.
Thoughtcrime, they called it. Thoughtcrime was not a thing that
could be concealed forever. You might dodge successfully for a while,
even for years, but sooner or later they were bound to get you.

Repression of thought, of ideas, of dissonance. Fact or fiction?

But worse was to come in 1950, for it was the year when the first credit card was introduced! Since then, so many of us have fallen foul of the ubiquitous 'hole in the wall' that so kindly dispenses money we don't have. It's a great system. At least most wives seem to think so.

However, in one respect at least, the British found their senses again and come 1951, we had good old Winston back in residence at Number 10 and, no doubt due to his efforts, (after all he had, almost single-handedly, won the Second World War), colour TV was introduced. Although if you were anything like me, it was many years before it took pride of place in our living room.

Color television! Bah, I won't believe it until I see it in black and white.

Samuel Goldwyn – always to be relied upon for originality!

And so came the year in Britain that did more for the sales of television sets than any brilliant marketing plan could ever have achieved. Princess Elizabeth became Queen at the tender age of 25 and they televised it for all her subjects to see. Queen Elizabeth did more for the growth and development of television in the UK than any other person, corporation or marketing programme, ever. And, I bet no-one gave her any commission!

The following year saw the conquest of Everest, a truly great achievement for mankind, especially considering the primitive equipment Edmund Hillary and Tenzing Norgay had with them, both instantly becoming the greatest heroes for all the youth of Britain and much of the world. We all went out and bought hiking boots and ropes.

On and up they stumbled, like flies on a whitewashed wall. An unmapped ice ridge stopped them, as it had stopped Team No.1. On one side, the ridge's gables projected over a face that fell 12,000 ft. Opposite was snow, firm enough for footholds, but guarded by a sheer rock face, 40 ft. high and holdless. At sea level this would be a minor obstacle to a trained mountaineer, but at 29,000 ft., neither Hillary nor Tenzing could attempt it. Instead they found a chimney that opened to the top. Hillary went first and crabbled his way upward through the chimney, using shoulders and knees as levers. Then it was Tenzing's turn, and soon the pair lay together in the frozen snow at the top. They got up and plodded on. As fast as one hump was cleared, the next blocked the view. Both men were slowing down when suddenly it loomed into view—one last narrow snow ridge running up to a peak beyond which nothing was higher. Bear Hug. They made it, roped together, and stood on the roof of the world. It was exactly 11:30 a.m. on Friday, May 29, 1953. Gravely they shook hands, and Tenzing, forgetting formality, hugged Hillary like a bear. Then they took photographs of the British, Nepal, Indian and U.N. flags lashed to Tenzing's icepick. What did it feel like to be there? Said Hillary: 'Damn good.' Tenzing, a devout Buddhist, said: 'I thought of God and the greatness of His work.' After 15 minutes' exposure, both were weakening rapidly. They started down and arrived, half frozen, at Camp VII. At first neither could speak, but their comrades forgave them that. On both bearded faces, festooned with icicles, a broad grin told the story that Everest at last had yielded to men who accepted the challenge because it was there

Excerpt courtesy of TIME magazine

Then, the next year came our flying doctor, Roger Bannister himself, breaking for Britain and the world, the four-minute mile. So we all pawned our climbing boots for running shoes; (we called them pumps in those day) and off we raced.

But I do remember another hero, James Dean, tragically dying so young, in a car accident in 1955:

> *An actor must interpret life, and in order to do so must be willing to accept all the experiences life has to offer. In fact, he must seek out more of life than life puts at his feet*

> *Dream as if you'll live forever. Live as if you'll die today*

So young to have said and done so much. So prophetic, and so deadly accurate.

So, at the tender age of ten in the year of 1956, what did I experience? What are my memories? I recall not being happy in the Cubs; I think it was to do with the very aggressive, mustachioed lip, overweight female leader, who would have done a great job in the Hitler youth camps. But I loved the Boy Scouts, especially when they made me Patrol Leader of a new patrol, so I was able to choose its name. I named it Panther Patrol. A black swift and courageous animal; the epitome of grace and physical superiority. My patrol (and I) never quite matched up to the name, I fear; but I loved being 'the Boss', - loved it even more when they made me Troop Leader; and that was over the Scout Master's own son, who was the same age as me. Was I an insufferable prat? Do you even require an answer? He was the first person in my life to really hate me; with absolute justification, I may say:

> *It is better to be hated for what you are than to*
> *be loved for something you are not.*

So advises Andre Gide, the French writer, humanist and moralist. But was he correct?

Elvis entered my life that same year with 'Heartbreak hotel', his own first entry into the music charts in the US, - the rest, as they say, is history. Colossal success and quality as an artist matched with massive failure as a human being. But still today he is 'The King', wherever you go, anywhere and everywhere in the world. There are Elvis impersonators outside the gates of Graceland and in Tokyo parks and in Tiananmen Square and in Red Square and in the pubs of London, Phuket and Prague. Incredible. There has just never been anyone who has come anywhere close to him in fame. Isn't that just unbelievable? In more than 60 years, no-one even remotely close, wow! I once started counting the number of his songs that were produced under the RCA label. I gave up when I got to 794!

> *Are you lonesome tonight,*
> *do you miss me tonight?*
> *Are you sorry we drifted apart?*
> *Does your memory stray to a brighter sunny day*
> *When I kissed you and called you sweetheart?*
> *Do the chairs in your parlor seem empty and bare?*

Do you gaze at your doorstep and picture me there?
Is your heart filled with pain, shall I come back again?
Tell me dear, are you lonesome tonight?

(words & music by Roy Turk and Lou Handman)

However, 1956 was also worthily marked, for those in the know, as being the 2,000[th] anniversary of the assassination of Julius Caesar; - bet you're really happy to realise that:

Let me have men about me that are fat;
Sleek-headed men and such as sleep o' nights;
Yond' Cassius has a lean and hungry look;
He thinks too much: such men are dangerous.

Shakespeare Act1 Scene 2 Line 192. As one becomes rounder and heavier with age, one appreciates this speech the more.

But there were also many nutters around in 1956, Egyptian leader Gamal Nasser being a prime example, (although perhaps not to the Egyptians), especially when he nationalized the Suez Canal and became universally hated by most of the civilized world. Ships in the desert now closing rather than opening a life-line so many depended upon for their very existence. Then, in the same year, came the plaintive cry to be hauntingly heard nightly on the radio:

Hungary calling; Hungary calling

I remember it as one of the most desperate pleas for pity and help that I've ever heard in my life; largely to go ignored as the Russian tanks began their rape of that proud country. A country striving to climb through its poverty into a state that might be able to manage its own affairs and to really care for its people. A care so much better than the evil Communist godfather. More than 250,000 people fled the country during the uprising whilst thousands of their brethren were left behind to die at the hand of the rabid communists; meanwhile the swaddled Brits complained about petrol rationing resulting from the Suez crisis and switched off their radio sets. The plaintive appeals went unanswered.

As a businessman in Russia

and in China…

As a teacher in Tonga

and Mozambique

As a sailor in Hong Kong

and in Singapore

As John Proctor in Arthur Miller's The Crucible

As Sir Toby in Twelfth Night, *with my son, Stafford playing Feste, the clown. He got better reviews than me, – damn!*

When, finally I did get to Hungary I was approaching thirty years old and it was there on Lake Balaton and on the river Danube, (referred to as The Duna in Hungary) that my business associate and friend, Bela Juhasz, taught me to water ski behind his wholly capitalistic ski boat. He also owned an ancient and beautifully preserved light blue diesel Mercedes that purred along the potholed and dimly lit roads of Budapest. Bela's greatest love was to have a complete understanding, word by individual word, of every record in his collection, especially those by Frank Sinatra and Ella Fitzgerald. Not only did I have to rapidly gallop through my vague recollection of the lyrics I was hearing, I also had to explain vagaries of the English language, many of which didn't make much sense as they were forced rhymes to meet the cadence of the music. 'My Way' was easy in comparison with 'Straighten up and fly right'. I loved the Hungary of the 1970's, a non-communist country but with a Communist government, a delightfully sprightly musical ambience pervading the many restaurants, all serving the same dishes, especially the hot nourishing Hungarian Goulash soup. My favourite Hungarian proverb of the time, which expressed what I felt about that whimsical city with its fairy castle battlements was:

May you live a thousand years, and I, a thousand less one day; that I might never know the world without you.'

But times have a dreadful habit of changing

Many was the evening I strolled or even jogged (I was much younger and more foolish in those days) along the river bank from the Duna Intercontinental Hotel to the Parliament buildings strangely modelled after the mother of all parliaments in the UK. Occasionally I would be approached by a courteous young man and asked if I would like to change some of my hard currency into local currency (the Forint). Of course, I followed all the then instructions of the British government and did not do so; that is until my second visit when I soon wised up. I was to visit that delightfully culturally complete city on a monthly basis for almost 4 agreeable years. In 2004 I returned to display its treasures to Athena. They had almost all been destroyed by wanton capitalism and we were strongly advised not to walk along the river side of the Duna after ten-o-clock in the evening. This time I took the warning and complied. The city had dried up and died and grave dangers lurked in the shadows that never existed under the repressive Communist regime. Progress?

I was ten years old when Mel Gibson and Tom Hanks were born. Shit! Doesn't that age one? Who wouldn't have wanted to be and do what they have done? Envy is a terrible force. Although, on the bright side, Velcro was invented this year - goody. And so, I take solace in the fact that it will be in use well after Mel and Tom (and me) have been planted or burnt.

Your modern teenager is not about to listen to advice from an old person, defined as a person who remembers when there was no Velcro.'

This from Dave Barry - American writer and humorist

In 1958, Chinese Leader Mao Zedong launched the 'Great Leap Forward' and Hula Hoops became popular – obviously the two events are linked, I just have to work out how.

Wooden Hula Hoops were introduced in Australian stores in 1957 after they proved to be a popular exercise tool in schools. Richard P. Knerr and Arthur K. Melvin of Wham-O, a fledgling California toy manufacturer, soon took notice of the Hula Hoop craze and began selling plastic hoops in the United States. Within four months, twenty-five million Hula Hoops had been sold!

Nothing much seemed to happen in my life from then until 1962 when the Cuban Missile Crisis began; this was great fun. Shall we, shan't we? Go in, stay out? What's the latest? We were treated to many 'wise' words from JFK:

My fellow citizens: let no one doubt that this is a difficult and dangerous effort on which we have set out. No one can foresee precisely what course it will take or what costs or casualties will be incurred. Many months of sacrifice and self-discipline lie ahead – months in which both our patience and our will be tested – months

86

in which many threats and denunciations will keep us aware of our
dangers. But the greatest danger of all would be to do nothing

How many times have words and phrases such as these been employed by world leaders to justify war?

But, in reality, the event that stole the headlines and even the activity of JFK was the stunning, sudden and most mysterious death of Marilyn Monroe, she of the electric body parts, the simple (very) wit and the squeaky voice. Beloved by millions, some, quite some, more intimately than others. One of these, very high profile 'others' was to join her in death but one year later. Only the good die young, they say.

So, 1963 was the year the world said goodbye to JFK, the great white hope and dream of America, and it took until the advent of Bill Clinton to at last bring some charisma back into American life and politics. It took that long! But thank goodness they had Cassius Clay, now Muhammad Ali, to lift their collective spirits as he began to:

Float like a butterfly, sting like a bee

He swept all before him and gained the crown and accolades of becoming the most attractive World Heavyweight Champion of all time, before, during and since.

A rooster crows only when it sees the light. Put him in the dark
and he'll never crow. I have seen the light and I'm crowing.

And no-one denied him that crowing. Yet he was to be stripped of the title relatively soon thereafter for refusing to serve in the pointless Vietnam war which began this same year (1965) and lasted, it seems in retrospect, for ever; as indeed so too is Iraq, some 40 years on.

The following year two events occurred which, even to the simplest of minds, must in some way be interconnected; both were so outrageously absurd. One was the launch of Mao Zedong's cultural revolution, the other the launch of star ship 'Enterprise', - yes, 'Star Trek' came to town, vying for silliness, even tragic lunacy with Mao, who's contribution to this world is best described by Jung Chang (she of 'Wild Swans' fame) and her English husband, Jon Halliday in their absolutely astonishing and riveting book, 'Mao, - The Unknown Story' published in 2005. Hopefully the remnants of the red army faction cannot now reach them. They open our eyes and that of all historians to the reality that was Mao:

> *Mao shunned all constraints of responsibility and duty. 'People like me only have a duty to ourselves; we have no duty to other people. I am responsible only for the reality I know' He explicitly rejected any responsibility towards future generations. 'Some say one has a responsibility for history. I don't believe it. I am only concerned about developing myself, I have my desire and act on it. I am responsible to no one'. Absolute selfishness and irresponsibility lay at the heart of Mao's outlook. These attributes he held to be reserved for 'Great Heroes' – a group to which he appointed himself. For this elite he said, 'Everything outside their nature, such as restrictions and constraints, must be swept away by the great strength in their nature. When Great Heroes give full play to their impulses, they are magnificently powerful, stormy and invincible. Their power is like a hurricane arising from a deep gorge, and like a sex-maniac on heat and prowling for a lover... there is no way to stop them.'*

And no-one did stop him until he had killed, directly or indirectly well over 70 million people. This was more than all killed in the Second World War. He took joy in upheaval and destruction:

> *Long lasting peace is unendurable to human beings, and tidal waves of disturbance have to be created in this state of peace*

He certainly created these tidal waves, even more destructive to humanity than the worst that nature can offer. How can his picture still proudly hang in Red Square?

In December of 1967 the world saw the first ever heart transplant performed by Dr. Chris Barnard in South Africa, while the following year the hearts of Martin Luther King Jr. ('I have a dream') and

Robert F. Kennedy were stilled forever by two of the world's madmen. The following year, however, saw Americans dancing on the moon:

This is one small step for a man, one giant leap for mankind

Words recited by Neil Armstrong as he became the first man to walk on the surface of the moon, just about the same time as pipe smoking, ketchup spreading Harold Wilson put his feet under the table in 10 Downing Street. Remarkable!

Such an unremarkable man in such a remarkable job and he hung on to it for so long, doing so despite almost universal distrust in him as a person and in his policies as a leader. Thank goodness for Dennis Healy who brought some quodos, acceptability and trust into a bewilderingly unstable government, - that went on for years! – My Dad was in it, so I have a bit of an inside story. It's frightening what went on behind closed doors, and you think Blair is bad; - he's an angel in comparison. Here's one from Harold that typifies Harold:

Courage is the art of being the only one who knows you're scared to death. The main essentials of a successful prime minister are sleep and a sense of history

But we cannot leave 1966 without remarking on the greatest single event in English history since Harold (the other one) got the arrow in his eye. Yes, we all know, England crushed Germany again, (third time that century!) in the greatest of all battles, The FIFA World Cup. Our lads beating the Huns 4-2 (after extra time). Oh bliss! Everyone in Britain remembers where they were that day, there was only one place to be, the world stood still while we all watched, spellbound and proud. Do you remember their names?

Gordon Banks, George Cohen, Jackie Charlton, Bobby Moore (Captain), Ray Wilson, Nobby Stiles, Alan Ball, Bobby Charlton, Martin Peters, Geoff Hurst, Roger Hunt with (Sir) Alf Ramsy as Coach

West Germany's team? Who on earth wants to know! Let's re-live a little of the glory:

With eleven minutes of extra time gone, Alan Ball put in a cross and Geoff Hurst's shot from close range hit the underside of the cross bar, bounced down - apparently on or just over the line - and was cleared. The referee Gottfried Dienst was uncertain if it was a goal and consulted his linesman, Tofik Bakhramov from the USSR, who in a moment of drama indicated that it was. After non-verbal communication, as they had no common language, the Swiss referee awarded the goal to the home team. The crowd and the audience of 400 million television viewers were left arguing whether the goal should have been given or not.

England's decisive third goal has remained controversial ever since the match. According to the Laws of the Game the definition of a goal is when the whole of the ball passes over the goal line

In England, supporters cite the good position of the linesman and the statement of Roger Hunt, the nearest England player to the ball, who claimed it was a goal and that was why he wheeled away in celebration rather than tapping the rebounding ball in.

However, in Germany it is commonly believed that the goal was given incorrectly, with the President of Germany Heinrich Lübke being an exception to this rule. He stated 'The ball was in', which was criticised as one of the embarrassing mistakes he made during his final term

One minute before the end of play, the West Germans sent their defenders forward in a desperate attempt to score a last-minute equaliser. Winning the ball, Bobby Moore picked out the unmarked Geoff Hurst with a long pass, which Hurst carried forward while some spectators began streaming onto the field and Hurst scored moments later. Hurst later admitted that his blistering shot was just an attempt at sending the ball as far into the Wembley stands as possible in order to kill time on the clock

The final goal gave rise to one of the most famous sayings in English football, when the BBC commentator Kenneth Wolstenholme described the action:

And here comes Hurst, he's got... some people are on the pitch, they think it's all over. It is now! It's four!

The final was the most watched event ever on British television, attracting 32.60 million viewers.

But sadness was to follow this success as unbelievably The (illustrious) Beatles played their very last concert at Candlestick Park in San Francisco, California. I blame the actor Ronald Reagan, he was elected 3 months later as Governor of the state of California; he simply could not handle the competition and, in some clandestine way, managed to get them to fall apart. The CIA has a long reach, my friends.

There wasn't anyone of any importance born in this year, but the world lost Kathleen Norris, American writer (born 1880) Buster Keaton, American actor and film director (born 1895) Hedda Hopper, American gossip columnist (born 1885) – not really much of a loss, and Walt Disney, (born 1901)

In 1971 London Bridge was transported to the US and the UK changed to the decimal system for currency; these events sounding the death knell for much of what we cherished as Britishness. The rot had set in. So too in the US, as the revelations of 'Tricky Dickie' and his Watergate shenanigans began to surface. The world watched, laughed and cried, and buried heads in the sand. But at least there began the severe questioning of the war in Vietnam, which led to the US pull-out in 1973 and the resignation of Dickie in 1974.

At the maturing age of 30 in 1976 I was to witness, with pride, the first commercial flight of Concord and the resignation of Harold Wilson; while our revered Monarch sent the first royal e-mail. To whom? Oh, and delight over more delight, the UK won the Eurovision song contest with the superlative, 'Save your kisses for me', sung by The Brotherhood of Man. What an innocent time it now appears; when such a song could sweep the world! – Oh lost youth.

The preeminent events of 1976? Unquestionably the death of Mao and the appointment of an ever smiling peanut farmer to the position as President of the United States (no wonder he was smiling). As Louis Armstrong was heard to croon:

What a wonderful world!

Nobody important – at least not yet, - was born in this year but we said farewell to Agatha Christie, Paul Robeson, Howard Hughes (no comment) and sadly, before his time, the rancidly attractive comedian, Sid James, he of 'Hancock' and 'Carry-On' fame.

But the next year was the worst. Elvis found dead; we all know where. How truly sad.

A world event that for sadness can only be compared to the appointment of Margaret Thatcher as first female Prime Minister of Great Britain in 1979, but although she lasted far too long in the job, our memory of Elvis and the pleasure he gave to countless millions, lives on and grows deeper, while thankfully hers diminishes year by year.

I am extraordinarily patient, provided I get my own way in the end

Was she really attempting humour when she said this? She was never known for her spontaneous hilarity. She was more recognised for statements such as:

If you want to cut your own throat, don't come to me for a bandage

She really comes across as endearing, doesn't she, and someone you would truly seek out as a leader of the modern world. – Not a question by the way. But she'll probably always be remembered for telling us that:

What Britain needs is an Iron Lady

A true contradiction in terms, surely even she understood that? Or maybe, as we leave her, we are best to remember one of the most telling of her comments:

You don't tell deliberate lies, but sometimes you have to be evasive

John Mortimer in his continuing autobiography, published in 1994 and entitled, 'Murderers and Other Friends' was, interestingly, for such an 'upper crust' person, a life-long Socialist, who had very little warmth for the Iron Lady and for what she was doing to Britain, he recalls:

The eighties brought a curse which some people called prosperity. It was the age when self-respect went with two cars and owning your own house; if you had less than these minimum requirements you might well be living in a cardboard box. House prices in our valley spiralled to dizzy height; a cottage with a leaking roof and a handkerchief of a garden could cost as much as a sizeable London house. Motorways were built and seemed in instant need of repair. Market towns, which had boasted wide streets, Georgian town halls and ancient churches were developed, operated on and degutted. Dreary and lifeless pedestrian precincts and shopping centres were inserted like useless pacemakers into their hearts. In such centres the wind blew empty Coca-Cola tins among concrete pots in which shrubs died, and the shops sold nothing anyone might want – such as fish, meat or ironmongery – but specialized in 'gifts', padded coathangers and embroidered knicker-bags, and greeting cards. These shops rapidly went bankrupt and the pedestrian precincts became places where the outcasts of the monetarist society might urinate and sleep, or where the pupils from the local polytechnic, now called a university, could deal in more or less harmless drugs

With gritted teeth, however much she destroyed the soul of Britain, I must give it to Maggie for the way she handled the Falkland crisis in 1982; she was right, she was strong and firm and she displayed great powers of leadership. There, gulp, I said it! Mind you, the Cabbage Patch Dolls became stunningly popular at the same time. Is there a link I've missed?

We lost John Lennon to another of the world's crazed people in 1980, just at the time that Ted Turner created CNN and the year before THE fated Royal Wedding was watched by millions, even quite a few on Ted's new network. What else was to be discovered sunk?

Do you recall the finding of the 'unsinkable' Titanic in 1985, so many years after it did actually and completely, sink?

The story of the Titanic and the iceberg has grown into a legend of the sea. It took her discovery in 1985 to begin to find the truth behind the myth. On April 10, 1912, the RMS Titanic set sail from Southampton on her maiden voyage to New York. At that time, she was the largest and most luxurious ship ever built. At 11:40 PM on April 14, 1912, she struck an iceberg about 400 miles off Newfoundland, Canada. Although her crew had been warned about icebergs several times that evening by other ships navigating through that region, she was traveling at near top speed of about 20.5 knots when one grazed her side.

Less than three hours later, the Titanic plunged to the bottom of the sea, taking more than 1500 people with her. Only a fraction of her passengers were saved. The world was stunned to learn of the fate of the unsinkable Titanic. It carried some of the richest, most powerful industrialists of her day. Together, their personal fortunes were worth $600 million in 1912! In addition to wealthy and the middle class passengers, she carried poor emigrants from Europe and the Middle East seeking economic and social freedom in the New World.

One fact I'm not sure I should share with you is that the captain of this ill-fated vessel and thereby the clump that is ultimately responsible for its early demise in a watery grave, came from my home town. Oh! Captain Edward John Smith - Oh yes, the captain of the ill-fated Titanic was a Stoke-on-Trent man. Born in Hanley (or some say it's Etruria) on 27th January 1850. He went on to enjoy an illustrious naval career which came, of course, to an abrupt end on the 15th April 1912 when he sunk the unsinkable and himself with her.

So now I've reached the age of 40 and, as far as I can see, I'm in Asia for the remainder of my life and the year is 1986. I'm remarried and have been given a dowry of two Great Danes, one that squats and pees whenever it sees me, two step-kids who hate me for usurping the role of their natural father, all grandly compensated for by a great job, wife, car, ocean going yacht and terrific lifestyle. But my two sons also were suffering, far away in England at Abbotsholme

Public School in Staffordshire, and there was little I could do; little I did do. Often as I look back on my life, this has been a source of regret to me. Perhaps I should have fought for them to remain with us in Asia, no matter the pain. But hedonism is an integral part of the human psyche and I have my fair share of it.

However, there is salvation for all of us for this was the year, as you will of course all remember, when National Hugging Day was first observed. You mean you've forgotten. Gosh! It's held on January 21st every year and, as far as I know, it hasn't been cancelled yet. So make a big note in your diary and get hugging!

A poll in 2006 by Batchelors, the famous 'Hug in a Mug' has revealed that two out of three UK adults have a hug at least once a day. The Scots are the most frequent huggers with 26% of them hugging more than five times a day with Londoners not far behind with 24% enjoying at least five cuddles daily. The Welsh are not so touchy feely however, with 10% of the respondents in Wales sadly never receiving hugs.

But they can't half sing!
Very few people in Japan or Korea hug, what does that tell us, I wonder.

As with 1976, nobody important was born in 1986 but excellent singer and actor, and apparently, very nice man, Michael Crawford, he of 'Some Mothers do 'ave 'em' and 'The Phantom of the Opera' fame was made an Officer of the British Empire (what's left of it) and we lost the great actor and personality, James Cagney, at the grand age of 87 and a somewhat younger Cary Grant at 82, all outlived by distinguished old statesman, our friend and mentor, Harold Macmillan, who made his last speech at the age of 92. I liked Harold. Old school, old style, but something about him you just had to respect. Perhaps it was his dog-like bleary eyes, betraying a stolid depth within.

In the year (1989) that President Bush, - the first one; (fancy the world being blessed by two from the same stable. Just fancy!) - made the earth shaking revelation that, (unbelievably), was widely reported:

And so, on hearing this news and because of one or two other equally modest events, the Berlin Wall was demolished. A great scourge among mankind took its last fall. The border had cut through 192 streets, 97 of them leading to East Berlin and 95 into the GDR. At least 100 people were killed at the Berlin Wall, the last of them was Chris Gueffroy on the 2nd June 1989.

The BBC was ecstatic in its reporting, but then, so was everyone else:

> *At midnight on 9th November, East Germany's Communist rulers gave permission for gates along the wall to be opened after hundreds of people converged on crossing points. They surged through, cheering and shouting and were be met by jubilant West Berliners on the other side. Ecstatic crowds immediately began to clamber on top of the wall and hack large chunks out of the 28-mile (45-kilometre) barrier.*

And not so far away, a great defender of people's rights and privileges, Lech Walesa became the first president of Poland. Funny how much he reminded me of Harold Wilson. Was it the clothes, the stature, the way he walked? The trust level we should have in him?

Nelson Mandela was freed this same year of 1990 and went on to become the first black President of South Africa:

> *During my lifetime I have dedicated myself to this struggle of the African people, I have fought against white domination, and I have fought against black domination. I have cherished the ideal of a democratic and free society in which all persons live together in harmony and with equal opportunities. It is an ideal which I hope to live for and to achieve. But if it needs be it is an ideal for which I am prepared to die*

A year later came the collapse of the Soviet Union. Macmillan's 'wind of change' had reached gale proportions.

So now I'm 50 and it's 1996. John Howard begins what will prove to be a long and successful tenure as Prime Minister of Australia and Dolly the Sheep becomes the first successfully cloned mammal (and so many of us believed it was the younger Bush that held this honour). She to live to the ripe old age of 7, Bush still with us. Is their really justice in the world?

This year also saw the infamous Osama bin Laden writing 'The Declaration of Jihad on the Americans occupying the country of the Two Sacred Places,' his first open call for war and the world began to discover another form of madness.

However, in order to retain our perspective we must also recall that 1996 was the year in which the world-renowned bird expert Tony Silva was sentenced to 7 years in prison without parole, for leading an illegal parrot smuggling ring.

> *He's not pining, he's passed on. This parrot is no more. He has ceased to be. He's expired and gone to meet his maker. He's a stiff, bereft of life, he rests in peace. If you hadn't have nailed him to the perch he'd be pushing up the daisies. He's rung down the curtain and joined the choir invisible. This is an ex-parrot!*

If you don't know where this quote comes from then you have missed one of the very best events of the 20th Century!

We lost nimble Gene Kelly, loquacious Stirling Silliphant and magical Ella Fitzgerald, as well as the two great British comic talents of Leslie Crowther and Willie Rushton, the later only making it to the age of 59 before shuffling off this mortal coil. Another non sixty-year-old.

And Mad Cow Disease hit Britain; just before the moment when Hong Kong was given back to China. Two events interminably interlinked.

However, perhaps an even more obvious linkage may be found in 1998 when Viagra came onto the market for the first time and US

President Bill Clinton was impeached. Thankfully he beat the idiots that impeached him and doubled his order for Viagra; what a hero!

I didn't inhale and never tried it again

Ten years later, in 2006 the first successful penis transplant (in China) was achieved. I make no judgement, but my comment would be that I hope they matched size and matter, for size does matter and I've been in the showers with very many Asians and a lot of them are bow-legged enough. This was also the year in which US Vice President Dick Cheney accidentally shot his friend and lawyer, Harry Whittington in the face with a shotgun. What a dick!

In March of 2006, my 60th year, we saw the ban on smoking in public places such as bars and restaurants come into effect in Scotland. Scotland, of all places! Robbie Burns is turning over, wondering whether they will ban drinking in bars soon. Perhaps we should note that this year also saw the extinction of the Chinese River dolphin, - the Baiji – as extinct as smoking in Scottish bars.

But the best extinction was that of Saddam Hussein, although it was rather mucked up a bit; or was it?

By December of my 60th year, According to the Met Office, England experienced its warmest year since records began in 1659 with an average temperature of 10.82 degrees Centigrade. - WOW!

No births mattered in this year but who did we lose? John Profumo, remember him. Great chap, who parted from us at the age of 91, having left behind the only sex scandal to bring down a British government; It was really juicy fun at the time and had all the elements of show girls, spies and politicians. Roll over 007; you are far too tame by comparison. Although he does have:

All new partners, no condoms, no birth control, no consequences at all

As James was prone to say, at least once:

World domination. The same old dream. Our asylums are
full of people who think they're Naploeon. Or God.

But there's just not enough politicians safely ensconced within them

As one reaches 60, one begins to see many friends moving on; some like Gene Pitney and Freddie Garrity (Freddie and the Dreamers – remember?), who didn't even know they were my friends, and another Freddie, that of great bowling fame. The overwhelming Fred Truman; larger than life, both on and off the field of play. But a really sad and terribly premature departure was that of the Australian environmentalist and television personality, Steve Irwin, who was killed by a sting ray at the tender age of 44, with so much left to give, whether hunting crocs, playing with snakes or saving the environment. A man with more passion for animals than anyone of his generation. From one Eulogy:

Irwin became known throughout the world for his supreme love of reptiles, his huge and enthusiastic arm gestures, and his catchphrase ('crikey!'). A trademark move was to hunt down one of the huge saltwater crocodiles that inhabit the rivers and beaches of the Outback in Australia's tropical north, leap onto its back, grabbing its jaws with his bare hands, and then tie the animal's mouth with rope.

Irwin appeared to be a total lunatic, but a lunatic of the very best kind -- he pursued with full gusto the things he loved doing. And, who knew? The majority of the profits he received from his television work went to buying enormous tracts of land for use as conservation space.

"I am shocked and distressed at Steve Irwin's sudden, untimely and freakish death," Australian Prime Minister John Howard said. "It's a huge loss to Australia."

So what do we have to look forward to, those of us now entering our 61st year in the 21st Century? More mobile phones to usurp our cherished silences. Already 80% of the world land surface has coverage by cellular networks and usage approaches 100% in developed countries with India and China playing fast catch up. Ugh!

I guess we must also look forward to ever increasing conflicts and civil unrest around this world of ours, I certainly don't see it diminishing. Just look at some of what we have today:

- Sri Lanka civil war (1983-present)

- War in Afghanistan (2001-present)

- Darfur conflict (2003-present)

- Civil war in Iraq (2006-present)

- North Korean nonsense

- Central African War (2006-present)

- War in Somalia (2006–present)

I guess I've easily missed quite a few and would rather continue to do so.

Overpopulation continues as does poverty, as does global warming, - go see the icebergs *now*; as does AIDS, as does bird flu, all still without cures or vaccines; but we still have:

- Rowan Atkinson, - most commonly known, from the North Pole to the South, for his universal humour as Mr. Bean

- Elton John – he was so much better when he was younger (not true of many other 60 year olds)

- Bob Geldof – I have never liked him, but I respect him

- Shakira, music artist and humanitarian – she just looks so good!

- Steven Spielberg, - director of Jaws, E.T. and Jurassic Park and what else to come?

- And YOU and ME!

Rock on!

As a lover, anywhere!

Me as Shakespeare

***Me as Chairman of the all girls Sudbury County
Netball League, - what a trial!***

The ones that didn't get away!

XI

I drink too much – wine that is; except for the three months that I gave up, actually this year (2007), as a bet with my eldest son, Stafford. The reciprocation being that he gave up smoking. He needed to, but of course I didn't!

How do I know it's too much?
Two reasons; the screaming left lobe headache the following day and the accursed doctor who gives me my annual physical and analyses my liver function.

'I suggest no more than half a glass of wine per day, Mr. Cant.'

Who the hell ever drank only half a glass of wine per day? Half a bottle I might understand and even manage, sometimes, but half a glass! – How did he ever pass his finals with such a nonsensical view of the human physiology and life and the living?

I came to alcohol rather late in life and, as I recount this story I will just open a bottle of Shiraz to help me along; basic plonk from Australia called 'Yellow Tail' – actually quite good, especially if you allow it to breathe for a while. Open it at midday to drink in the evening, - if you can be such a 'good' person!

Late in life for me was around the age of 26, when I was in Moscow in minus 30 degrees centigrade. The children in the streets looked like large round brown balls, completely swathed in layer upon layer;

totally unrecognizable as human beings. It was difficult, almost impossible for much of the time, to see where the orifice was that the tiny breaths came from as everything was so entirely muffled. I remember going for a pee in a public lavatory and, as with my fellow men standing in steaming line, I refused to remove my mittens and brave the intense cold. There were one or two unfortunate spillages. All thumbs. It went back in very quickly indeed; it didn't have a mitten.

Back to the initiation with de booze.

The hotel room was something less than appealing on my first visit to Moscow (actually, they changed but little in the three or four years I frequently visited there, despite constant changes of hotel, seeking the Holy Grail of some comfort, or something such). On the outside of many hotels and official buildings the architecture was dreadfully reminiscent of unbalanced Stalin's deranged wedding cakes. There was no heating, it was minus 30 in the streets; little warmer within. The bed had more and larger lumps than a grossly deformed camel. The bath had no plug. The water was warmish, never hot. The pipes clanked and gurgled, all day, all night. There was no room key provided and an insubstantial bolt on the inside of the bathroom door, no bolt on the door to the room.

I went downstairs. It was 1972. The service was indefensibly insolent, when any was provided at all; despite the fact that three people did one person's job; just so the propaganda machine could (truthfully?) proclaim that there was no unemployment in Mother Russia. My first time to Moscow I was ensconced in that hotel, The Ukrainia, for three weeks; attending business meetings during the day and chatteringly cold at night despite wearing just about all the clothes I had brought with me. I bought pajamas whilst in Russia for I never had the use for such garments at home. Once I put them on, I rarely took them off. I went to business meetings with a vest, underpants, two pairs of socks, (I couldn't get my shoes on with three), pajamas, shirt, tie, pullover, jacket and trousers, scarf, heavy overcoat, I bought myself a splendid Cossack hat from the 'duty free', Westerners only store in the hotel, that covered the ears and tied with a poofy bow under the chin and a pair of huge shammy-leather mittens. And I was still cold! At night I dressed down to the pajamas and, because I had been fully alcohol initiated by then, fell (often quite literally) into an untroubled pass-out sleep, neither knowing nor caring if I was warm or cold. But I did catch dreadful flu (they called it 'Asian' in those days), which remained with me for more than one month after I returned from Russia. Funny, I only noticed I had it when I got back to my home in Halstead, Essex.

The restaurant menu in the hotel (it was too cold to go out to try elsewhere; anyway, we were told our hotel was one of the best eating places in town!) never altered. Flat chicken, - well it didn't say 'flat' on the menu but that's what it was. Absolutely flat; the tiny bones crushed together into a minuscule piece of meat. Cold hard potatoes and an unspeakable and inedible cabbage type vegetable. Ice cream to follow, -if you could get a waiter to serve it to you. But, always, I mean always, local (sometimes rough, sometimes smooth) vodka was available. As available as drinking water, nay, more readily available.

One is forced to recall the words of Anthony Powell in a book that I can no longer find and thus cannot, sadly, give you the title of:

Dinner at the Huntercombe's possessed only two dramatic features.
The wine was a farce and the food a tragedy

There was nothing else for it; nothing else to do, no-where else to go, unless you wanted to freeze and die of lack of flat stringy chicks. Nothing except the warming balm of the vodka. A substitute for everything in life. For warmth, for decent food, for love, for sex, simply for everything. So the top came off and was thrown to the other side of the restaurant, where it would never be picked up by anyone, ever. In those days, maybe still today, no-one opened a bottle and replaced the cork or screw top. No matter what time of day it was. Perhaps they do still practice that engaging custom today. I have no burning desire to return to Moscow to find out.

One time I was appointed chairman of a symposium that started at 10:00 a.m. in one of the more famous hospitals in Moscow. I can even remember the subject matter – 'Electrophoresis as an accurate measurement of the incidence of myocardial infarction.' Spunky title wasn't it? Anyway, we had one American speaker from our company, myself as Chairman, an eminent physician from the hospital and some others. I had requested the main guys to meet in the 'eminent physician's' office at 09:00 so that I could (pedantically - as I was in those days) give my briefing to the speakers. Before I issued any more words than 'hello, thank you for coming', our Russian host had produced a bottle of (we found out later) excellent Vodka from his home state, complete with some blades of grass inside. Off the top came, grandly thrown to the other side of the office and he commenced to pour measures into three none too clean glasses on his desk. Nor were they thimble sized glasses. The bottle was consumed between the three of us by 09:45, - it was another cold day. So, damn me, he produced another, - after all, we still had fifteen minutes to go before we were 'on stage', and anyway, he reminded us: everything starts late in Russia. I think we began the symposium at around 10:30 and finished for lunch at around 13:30. I remember nothing past my introductory 'speech', -

'goo morninging every, hope you enjurour day.'

Benny Hill, our great and desperately lonely British comedian (they often are both) would have been well at home in this tiny office in this large Russian hospital, once Benny was asked:

'Do you want a drink?'
'It's too early.'
'What, too early for a drink?'
'No, too early for stupid questions. Of course I want a drink'.

I believe someone carried me to my bed that night, but not before we'd enjoyed a liquid lunch, a serious discussion about the joys of capitalism, this time our erudition washed down with ice cold afternoon beer, following which we consumed our obligatory flat chicken and a few more bottles of vodka, just because it was there.

That someone kindly took off my coat and shoes and covered me with my blanket. I awoke at around 3 a.m. cold and wondering about everything and everyone in the universe and, watching as the ceiling, spinning through its own vortex, finally forced me to have severe discussions, for quite a long time it seemed, with the great white ceramic echo chamber. But now, at last, I had discovered alcohol and began to work hard at making up for lost time and acquiring knowledgeable taste factors and adequate reasons for consumption. So much so that when, a few years ago, my wife and I, together with our Korean friends, went on a wine tasting holiday in South Africa, I was able to pontificate with the best and to compare with the worst. Thank you Mother Russia!

My new wine supplier, Steve Roberto, a chap with a very individual sense of humour, which hardly anyone understands, told me in May 2006,

> *Every glass of wine you have is an opportunity for*
> *enjoyment you may never have again.*

Lady Astor is often attributed with the following injudicious and intemperate offering, the response to which would have inevitably knocked her flat. But truly, in my limited research, I don't believe it was Lady Astor. Although it might just as well have been! One would have to pour through Hansard to verify exactly who it was. I have much better things to do with my next five years. Let us simply attribute it to a 'female MP', who was noted more for her strong independence of mind than for her beauty, when, turning on Churchill, after a rather heated exchange, foolishly declared:

> *'Mr. Churchill, you're drunk!'*
> *'And you, madam,' replied Churchill, 'are ugly.*
> *But I shall be sober tomorrow.'*

Gosh, I've just remembered where the quote about:

> *Won't you come into my garden; I would like my roses to see you*

comes from. Richard Brinsley Sheridan. Who else? – See what a glass (or two) of wine can do. And now I am also reminded of something I once told myself:

In my considered opinion, consciousness is not always advantageous

From my dear friends, Roz and Brian Colston, residents of Windsor Castle, comes the following gem, which they no doubt stole from someone else:

WATER – it has been scientifically proven that if we drink one litre
of water each day, at the end of the year we would have absorbed more
than one kilo of Escherichia coli bacteria found in faeces, in other words,
we are consuming one kilo of Doo Doo.
However, we do not run that risk when drinking wine (or rum,
whiskey, beer or other liquors) because alcohol has to go through a
distillation process of boiling, filtering and fermenting.
WATER = DOO DOO
WINE = HEALTH
Free yourself of Doo Doo, drink WINE! It is better to drink wine
and talk Doo Doo than to drink water and be full of shit.

Sometimes, oftentimes, it is good to bring sex and wine together; they are so often mutually advantageous; as Stirling Silliphant (what a glorious name!) opined in his novel 'Silverstar':

If the good Lord makes anything better than Singha
beer and Thai girls, he's keeping it to himself

My name and my ability with words are painfully lacking when compared with Stirling Silliphant but I strappingly believe:

Wine, especially red wine, is a gift. One that should always be
unwrapped around the tongue before lost in the swallow

But more importantly, let us begin to take our leave of this subject with the words of Umberto Eco from his 'Semiotics of theatrical performance' echoing in our ears:

*Who has said that to drink is bad? Who has said that the spectacle
of intoxication has to be interpreted as an ironical warning
and not as an invitation to the most orgiastic freedom?*

For, doesn't alcohol offer us a different sort of freedom? Freedom to
appreciate art and people and words, on a different plane, as it were.
Personally, I always write more fluently with a glass or three of wine
inside me; it's not an excuse, it's true. But if the glass or three becomes
four or more then I accept that the writing may deteriorate, even the
will to write weakens. Peter Mayle in his novel, 'Hotel Pastis', makes
another, equally valid observation about the power and potency of
wine:

*One of the pleasures of life, Simon thought, is the way women become
progressively prettier and more amusing the longer lunch lasts*

Moving on....

Now, what about MacDonald's and KFC and fried food, - I have an
(eldest) son who, sadly frequents such establishments, and so, even
more wretchedly, do his three siblings. I once, and constantly, have
to remind him that if I am ever so drunk or impecunious enough
to appear with him in such a place, then I have his permission
to completely disown him and anyone he communicates with who
might request the identity of his companion. He has agreed. Now,
as to fried food, John Cheever in his 'Oh, what a Paradise it seems'
glorifies fried food as follows:

*It was the smell of fried food that seemed to fill his consciousness. After
the discovery of love, the importance of hunting and the constancy of
the solar system came the smell of frying food. Even now, at the end of
the harvest in the most inaccessible of the Carpathians, the shepherds
come down from the mountains with their herds in the autumn to hear
gypsy fiddlers and a snareless drum and smell sausages rotating over
charcoal. It was barbarous, it disclaimed authority – and its magic
was malnutrition, acne and grossness. It was indigestible and highly
odourous and would be, if you were unlucky, the last thing you smelled
on your way to the executioner's block. And it was portable. You had*

111

*to be able to eat it as you sat in a saddle or rode on a ferris wheel or
walked the midways and alleys of some country fair. You had to be
able to eat it with your fingers picking it from a cornucopia of leaves or
bark or human skin while you paddled your war canoe or marched into
battle. They were eating fried food when they made the first human
sacrifice. Eggplant was being fried in the Coliseum when they broke
the philosopher on the wheel and fed the saints to the lions. They were
eating fried food when they hung the witches, quartered the pretender
and crucified the thieves. Public executions were our first celebrations
and this was holiday food. It was also the food for lovers, gamblers,
travellers and nomads. It was the food for spiritual vagrants.*

And you know what is the weirdest of all – MacDonald's really think
they invented fried food for the masses. Sad!

Some of the worst of food, of any nature, is to be found on the
areoplanes of the world, admittedly some airlines, especially in
Business or First Class are trying hard, but most still belongs in the
world as perceived by Peter Mayle, (hello Peter, once more) writing
in his enchantingly modest book, Hotel Pastis, as he was on his way
to France on that airline, you know the one...

*He shook his head at the stewardess who was offering plastic-
shrouded dinners to those in the terminal stages of hunger*

I wonder if most of the chefs for the airlines are female. I only wonder
this for I remember what Myrtle Reed had to say:

*Men make better cooks than women because
they put so much more feeling into it*

I have to agree with that. Who are the enthusiastic cooks on TV, in
the best hotels? - My case rests. Except there is a lot of truth in what
John Erskine has to say about cooking, and this may be where we
have the answer to the fast food and airline cuisine quality:

*All cooking is a matter of time.
In general, the more time the better.*

112

XII

One day I shall write what may be one of the shortest books in the world. Here are some of the chapter headings:

- *Sophisticated Australians*
- *Linguistic Russians*
- *Modest Americans*
- *Assertive Thais*
- *Gentle Koreans*
- *The patriotism of 21st century Englishmen*
- *Quiet Italians*
- *Proof that the French are not a snobbish race*
- *The erudite Israeli*
- *Clean Arabs*
- *Animal friendly Moslems*
- *Hard-working Brazilians*
- *Sweet-smelling Africans*
- *Honest Indians*
- *Tidy Chinese*
- *Smiley Japanese*

Do you have others?

XIII

SPORT: - Now, I'm not terribly competent at anything other than long distance walking, a lot of swimming and the odd (very odd) bicycle ride.

Sir Stanley Matthews, how I wish I'd met him, hailed from my own home town, Stoke-on-Trent and had the same birth date as my Father and was indisputably the greatest footballer of them all, even better than the enchanting Georgie Best *('I spent most of my money on fast cars fast women and booze and I wasted the rest')*, had this delightful story to recount in his autobiography, 'The way it was':

'Wilf', says Jimmy (the coach), 'You're up against Peter Broadbent today. 'I know, Jimmy. He's a great player and a great sportsman,' says Wilf, all a tremble. 'That's as maybe,' says Jimmy. 'Now, you come from a home with just your mum and your little sister, don't you?' says Jimmy. 'Yes, just me mum, me sister and me,' says Wilf 'And this being your professional football debut you want that winning bonus really badly, don't you, Wilf?' 'Yes, I do,' says Wilf. 'I know that, son,' says Jimmy. 'With your winning bonus I know you plan to buy your mother a new dress. Well, that Peter Broadbent, he's going out there today and he's going to do his utmost to stop you getting that winning bonus.. Your mother has brought you up well, she's worked hard and made sacrifices for you and your sister. She deserves a nice dress, but this Peter Broadbent doesn't want your mother to have it. 'And that little sister of yours,' says Jimmy, 'She needs a new pair of

114

shoes for school, I know that. Now, with your winning bonus today, you can buy her them shoes. But that Peter Broadbent, he doesn't want her to have them, Wilf. He wants to take those new shoes away from that little sister of yours. Are you going to let him do that, Wilf? 'No!' says Wilf, jumping up to his feet and going all red and misty with anger. 'Then make sure you get out there today and take the ball off him, Wilf,' says Jimmy. Just as Wilf emerges from the door of their dressing room, the first player he sees is Peter Broadbent carrying a ball. Now Peter, being the gentleman and sportsman he is, knows this is Wilf's debut so he stops and says, 'Good luck today, young man.' But Wilf, all hyped up, snatches the ball out of Peter's hands and shouts, 'Gimme that ball, you heartless thieving bastard!'

My brush with football lasted but two years, when, at the age of eleven I was head and shoulders above most other members of the opposing team, by twelve it was half a head, by thirteen I had been overtaken by almost all of the opposing forwards, so I gave football up as I was no longer taller and stronger than the rest of them. Time to retire. I began my career in Football as Right Back and I remember with affection being coached for two days by Danny Blancheflower (who?) in the vagaries of this important position on the field. Actually, it wasn't individual coaching, I was one of at least fifty (could have been one hundred) boys of around twelve years of age selected to learn at the feet of the maestro. I was selected because of my size, nothing more. Danny was a tall and charming Irishman, who, in the 1950's was signed by Aston Villa as a mid-field player and sufficiently strengthened the team to keep it out of relegation danger. But his real success was as a player for the Irish National team from 1950 to 1962 (a long time in football), when he gained 56 caps and even managed to score two goals. He was my hero for at least a month.

I enjoy stamina, non contact sports, especially after my experience of having been selected for the school first eleven for a couple of years (again because of my size) to play in the crashingly boring game of cricket as wicket keeper. I wore a box. It must have been a second-hand one. I was hit only once in the vitals and the box did bugger all to protect me. I was examining myself for weeks afterwards; wondering if I would ever be able to become a parent. I gave up cricket pretty soon after the 'home strike'.

I felt, at the time, much empathy with John Mortimer, who, when writing in his autobiography, 'Clinging to the Wreckage', has this to say:

> *Sport, I have discovered, fosters international hostility and leads the audience, no doubt from boredom, to assault and do grievous bodily harm while watching it. The fact that audiences at the National Theatre rarely break bottles over one another's heads, and that opera fans seldom knee one another in the groin during the long intervals at Covent Garden, convinces me that the theatre is safer than sport.*

No more to be said…

Is fishing a sport? 'Sacrilege!' some would cry, 'of course it's a sport!', and at one time, I am reliably informed, it used to draw more 'sportsmen' than does football (proper football that is, not the American grunt-without-grace game). Well, I'm not so sure myself, the only fishing I ever did was on Lake Kariba in Zimbabwe when, surrounded by hippos; myself and my Korean friend, Sun Gil Lee, stared jealously on as my wife caught the only (spiky and not at all appealing) fish of the afternoon's adventure! Perhaps she achieved this as a first time fisher, beginner's luck, whilst apparently remaining completely impervious to the undeniable fact that had we were drifting less than a very dangerous ten metres from a brutal hippo family.

My only other claim to fishing fame was when we were returning from a sail to the Philippines from Hong Kong on a friend's yacht, - he, David Kong, was (and probably still is) an avid fisherman. For almost one day (it seemed) he hung on while a sizeable Dorado tried to pull his arms from their sockets. Being David, always a leader, constantly competitive, he hung on, shouted instructions to others and left the running of the boat to Mark, who appeared distinctly disinterested in the entire experience; after all, it was cutting into sundowner time. Anyway, somewhere just north of The Thousand Islands (or was it only a hundred? – I can't remember,) - I was delegated the job of Gaffer. Now, I always thought Gaffers were guys in charge of things such as jails and building sites, - but no, - A Gaffer is the guy who swings and sticks the gaff (the deadly long hook on the end of a totally unmanageable wooden pole) directly into the proffered (some chance!) gills of the unobligingly oversized and under friendly monsters of the ocean.

Anyway, I gaffed. Made a total mess of it, lost the gaff overboard; luckily with Mark's skilled seamanship, recovered it and as David pulled and I stood and Mark steered and the girls whooped and as I was just about to strike, this bloody great head came rushing out of the sea towards me with such momentum that it piled itself on top of me, floored me into the well of the yacht and smothered me completely. I think someone said 'well gaffed, Howard', but I couldn't swear to it.

Once it and I had ceased our mutual writhings, I was able, with the help of the girls, - David was a mite weary and Mark had decided that if the sundowners were not to be consumed now, they never would be – I managed to truly insert the gaff into the gills for the obligatory photo. The fish was some two feet longer than me. I shuddered at its size, its power and its weight. But there was great sadness too, for the beautiful hues of blue and gold and green that had adorned his mighty scales as he fought his last battle, were, before my eyes, turning a cheerless grey.

We ate that fish, raw and cooked for four days. All six of us; then we had to throw it over the side, the smell was too bad. It was still quite a monster when we had to let it go.

I didn't want to go fishing again after that experience.

Kenneth Clark, author of 'Civilization', both the book and the TV series; is also remembered for many contributions to our fishy knowledge. Recorded in his autobiography, 'Another Part of the Wood', is his own fishing memento. He probably liked fishing, I guess:

But I must admit that the rare occasions when one does hook a salmon are worth waiting for. The whirling reel, the splendid curve of the

fish leaping out of the water as it makes for a waterfall, the terrible
moment when one's line begins to run out and one has to run up and
down the bank, sploshing into the stream – all this arouses a state of
mindless exhilaration which I suppose men used to feel in a cavalry
charge. From the humanitarian point of view it must be indefensible,
but it does seem to be connected with a deep and necessary human
instinct. There are few more harmless ways of experiencing the sense of
glory than by playing and landing a twenty-pound salmon, and it is
an interesting example of folk-philology that the ugly, short stick with
a lump of lead at the end of it with which this magnificent specimen
of the will to live is finally killed is known colloquially as a 'priest'

No, I'm afraid, still not for me. I stopped wanting to be Hemingway many years ago. The only creatures I have no difficulty in killing are mosquitoes, ants and cockroaches. That's it.

Have you ever been passed by speed skaters? They remind me of large graceful and powerful fish. It's quite a terrifying experience. I was trolling along quite nicely on my bicycle beside the river Han, which grandly bisects Seoul city and whoosh they blurred past! My immediate thoughts I instantly set down on a scrap of toilet paper, which I always carry; well, you never know…

The stimulating energy and graceful synergy of man and wife
power skating, one behind the other, seemingly only one; whooshing
along the concreted banks of the Han River is tough to surpass

Beautiful to experience, beautiful to watch, scary in its latent power. If *they* are so good, what on earth are the Olympic athletes capable of? Awesome!

XIV

Thoughts from abroad....

When I first landed in Russia I felt strange. Bizarre unhappy buildings, apparently designed to resemble grossly overdecorated wedding cakes; cheerless furniture and hideous cardboard-wooden kiosks for the immigration people, and suspicion. Everywhere there was total suspicion, and tangible concern. Intense trepidation not to be seen doing the wrong thing. Fear, almost, to do anything, anything at all. Then I met Gregor who did not seem to live up to his name. He was diminutive, but underneath, real tough. So maybe he did live up to his name. Eventually the secret police got him for phoning too frequently to London to reach an English girl he had fallen in love with when she was, for six months, an exchange student, teaching the English language at Moscow University. One time I brought him a sheepskin coat (a luxury he could never himself have afforded) from England and I had to wear it (difficult to disguise it as a package) on entry to Sheremetyevo airport. Of course it was far too small for me and I was grossly foolish in proudly smiling and displaying it to him as I spied him at the other side of the baggage retrieval, standing, seeking obscurity, nestling behind a cupboard behind a glass partition. When he saw me stupidly parading in his coat, he ran like a scared rabbit out of the building in case any official had seen and understood. Such a gift, in those days, the 1970's, would have resulted in his arrest, maybe my deportation. How stupid I was. Eventually, as I say, he was arrested, in 1974. I never saw or heard from him again. His crime, falling in love with an English girl to whom I occasionally conveyed letters from him. It was Christmas Eve 1974 when he called her to tell her he missed and loved her. On Christmas Day 1974 they arrested him and I never saw him again. I keep a freshly minted one rouble note from those days that I now have framed in my home. I call it Gregor and I don't ever really want to go back to Russia. I know it's changed and his sort of 'crime' no longer merits punishment; but oh, what a God-forsaken country it has now become. Mafia run, corruption abounding and an iron man at the helm who cannot or won't do anything about the country's dissipation. No, I really don't want to return. But I guess I will, just one more time, especially as Athena has never been there. Perhaps Gregor is still alive; perhaps I'll meet him again….Perhaps….there is a god?

Let's start fresh with Russia on some real help and some real reform

Jeffrey Sachs

Or perhaps it can never recover and must remain forever as the French philosopher; Emile Cioran saw it in the early 20th century:

Russia – immensity and suffocation

China was a totally different story. I never felt fear there; anger and hopelessness sure, but never fear. I guess I always felt 'superior'; a wonderfully overused yet undeniably useful trait of the English. (The non-English often don't agree.) However, my 'superiority' saw me through. I pushed my way through crowds; I treated immigration officials and hotel personnel with either pity or disdain. Once, I even told the foreign trade officials that their system was 'bloody stupid' (I was trying to import a company car into Beijing for the use of my people there). There was an angry and shocked silence that lasted, it seemed, for hours. The discussions were brought to an abrupt halt and it took me almost two years to get back into the room with those particular and very influential officials. I was a bloody stupid arrogant idiot. You just don't criticize the government of China. At least not in those days, the early 1980's. Perhaps not even today. Bloody stupid, I was. But I was really very frustrated and fed up with drinking gallons of green tea and listening to profound silences. And I didn't like the vegetable and body smells that every Chinese suffused within and without his blue uniform or dark clothes. Overwhelming frustration was my predominant feeling. Frustration at their system, at their inability to make decisions, at their necessity to toe the party line, at their total nonsensical propaganda and restrictive regulations relating to their own people and extending, in both subtle and unsubtle ways to all foreigners. Perhaps the fundamental changes now occurring may make the country more attractive, especially when an actress such as Joan Chen can tell us:

I'm going back to work in China. Chinese movies are getting
very strong now. I'm going…to work on a movie based on
a classical novel. I play a woman who loves decadence

Back to the roots. Wasn't China a country that always loved, even revered, decadence; save for the silly season that continued for the last 60 years of the 20th century when vicious little blue people waved shabby little red books and promulgated an impossible ideology formed by crackpot zealots? A mere blip in the history of this vast and ageless country.

What a false place Saudi was. Dubai too. False in soulness, false in openness, false in culture, false in sophistication. Real only in material things and female repression and arrogance and carelessness. Saudi more than Dubai. But maybe it's sour grapes, for it is a truism that:

A Saudi now has to be very unlucky, very stupid and lazy not to do well

Dubai was glitter and Saudi smelly, the people I mean. The smell of the Arabs is really unfortunate, but they do via for unpleasantness with many Indians and most Africans. Have you ever been in a queue in Heathrow terminal 3 for a flight to Nigeria? It's quite unbearable. You are forced into hoping that you might get <u>this</u> marginally sweeter smelling person sitting beside you for the long and smelly journey, rather than <u>that</u> one. 'Can I please have a smell-free person beside me?' You request as you check in. She understands, she is sympathetic but there is nothing she can do. Then you reflect; 'that poor young English girl has to stay behind that desk for the entire check-in process for all the people on the flight.' And she may have to do it day after day. I hope BA gives her a free perfume allowance and smell-danger money. There is an old Nigerian proverb that recommends:

Hold a true friend with both hands

No thank you.

Pakistan was the absolute pits, perhaps not quite as pitty as Calcutta in the 70's but not far off. I was in transit there one time and placed in a cell-like room in a so-called hotel adjacent to the airport. They locked the door from the outside! To protect ME, they said! Eventually I somehow got to sleep. Sheer exhaustion, I guess. Then, a minute later, it seemed, the intrusive Muslim call to prayer rebounded around the walls of my cell. What a country, what a religion! Colin Gibson, in a somewhat different context gave us the following; but he may well have hit the mark:

Our position is that we take our lead from the
Foreign and Commonwealth Office, the Pakistani
Government and the Pakistan Cricket Board

Well, one sensible voice out of three is not too bad, I suppose

Calcutta did not have the calls to prayer, but it did have dirty beds and rats in the restaurant (uncooked – the rats, I mean), but it also had soul and excitement and friendliness and servitude. All of the elements that are missing in Pakistan. I never ever want to go back to Pakistan, but India, well India, I'll return to. Not to the Taj, - been there, done that, but to the Bombay (sorry Mumbai) that I remember from the 1980's and to Delhi, which was always easy and fundamentally welcoming. Then on to Ahmedabad in Gujarat state where camel carts used to bound down the streets conveying everything from people to household goods. I wonder if they still bound along today, it seems such a long time since I was there. Yes, as I write this I feel an urge to return. India and Indians aren't at all bad. Winston Churchill had it right when he declaimed:

India is a geographical term. It is no more a
united nation than the Equator

Or, maybe, we can reflect upon a typical Indian proverb offering a not so welcome picture:

Under the mountains is silver and gold, But
under the night sky, hunger and cold.

Brazil, I found to be really disappointing. I was expecting glamour and sexiness and bright lights and warm people and fun, fun, fun. I found very little there of anything approaching any of these elements. Rather, I discovered traditional contempt for the tourist, rubbish strewn on sidewalks, unfriendliness, poor cuisine and takers. Many takers, few givers. I was really surprised. I was expecting to find a mirror image of the givers of Asia as both inhabit the same latitude, albeit thousands of miles from one another; but there was a total absence of the Thai and Philippino smile; of the grace of the Koreans or the sophistication and politeness of the Japanese, of the friendliness of the Indonesians, the innocence of the Vietnamese, the bonhomie of the Burmese. Instead I found crass Singaporeans. Yes, that's what I found in Brazil. I found Singapore, albeit a dirty and an inefficient one.

It's really difficult to come across a quotation about any aspect
concerning Brazil or Brazilians that does not contain a reference
to football. What does that tell us about this country?

How can one describe America? Gross? Grandiose? Gargantuan? Grasping? Gluttonness personified? Great? Gigantic? Gallant? Grotesque? Garrulous? Gaseous? Gaudy? Generous? Gloating? Glossy? Greedy. (no question mark required).
But not Genteel, nor Gentle, nor naturally Gifted, not Grateful nor Groovy, not Glorious nor Graceful or Gracious. Above all, not consistently Good and certainly not Guiltless. Not a place for me or

my family to live. Certainly not. And I've only hit the 'G's'! And, worse still, I can't remember from where I found the next quotation, apt though it may be.

America is like an unfaithful lover who promised us more than we got

Maybe George Harrison of The Beatles, had a real point when he said, as the Beatles first planned to tour The States in the 1960's;

America has everything, why should they want us?

Precisely because, George, they simply do not have everything; especially what you and Paul and Ringo and John had to offer.

Switzerland holds a special place in my heart. For it is where I first fell in love. Mount Riga, near Beckenried; amongst the sun-drenched slopes and darkened valleys. With the burbling streams and the pulsating fountains of Lucerne. Along the shaded forest pathways and with the love-songs of the early 1960's throbbing in my ears. I fell in love. 'There's a summer place' (Mantovani?) was 'our' song. I just wish I could remember her name. I think it might have been Margaret. But with undying love, we promised ourselves, one to the other, by the shores of the lake, then went back wistfully yet buoyant to the dormitories shared by our schoolmates, to whom we never disclosed our love. We even stole a kiss in the moonlight. That's all we stole. And we were all of 15 years old. Is the world different today? Is more stolen? I sincerely hope not. For the wholesomeness and the pain and the memory is pure. Forever pure. But I would like to be able to remember her name.... I just remember the gifts I bought for all my family; I actually stole two of them because I had run out of pocket money by then. Perhaps I'd bought one too many ice creams for 'thingy'. Anyway, I bought (or stole) the norm.

In Italy for thirty years under the Borgias they had warfare, terror, murder and bloodshed but they produced Michelangelo, Leonardo da Vinci and the Renaissance. In Switzerland, they had brotherly love; they had five hundred years of democracy and peace and what did that produce? The cuckoo clock.'

Orson Welles

Poland was grand and sad and full of huddling people and cigarette smells and large girls and substantial food and a sledge drawn by horses on the road to Gdansk, overtaking our car as Marchin Witkowski and I drove to our meeting in that distant port city where the downfall of communism, at least in Poland, had began. It was just like a scene from Dr. Zhivago. But now as then there was poverty and there were prostitutes everywhere, but there were also wonderful cakes and beer and drunkenness and much huddling together for warmth, almost all the time. Overwhelming was the pride the Polish people had, still have, in their history and culture. Still hugely apparent was the suffering and then the re-building of the old town destroyed by the Germans in the Second World War and all was balanced by the basic beauty of the people. A beauty that is within; for few are outwardly truly beautiful, for they are a little too inclined to rotundity. Rather, they are a handsome race. They possess a roundness of beauty that emanates from the soul, from the pride of being Polish, from the pride of surviving. Yes, I'd like to return to Warsaw. Soon.

We not only peacefully created unimaginable political changes in Poland, putting Polish people on a road to freedom and democracy, but also showed other nations of the former eastern bloc the possibility of correcting historic injustice.

This from Pope Benedict XVI.
Yes, I believe they did

Hungary was all violins and singing and great food and smart people and wonderful crystal glassware and cafes on the pavements and happiness amongst poverty. Today there is much less poverty, more graft and less security, but in the 1970's, Budapest was a safe and lovely city, with safe and lovely people, who led tough but honest lives; who enjoyed rather than exploited the tourist; who were kind and courteous. A disease has got to them today. Last time I went, perhaps in 1995, it was a changed place. I'm not so sure I want to return again. I'd like to remember it as it was when I was 30 years old and it was a joy to be there. A joy to wander by the river Duna and to watch the cargo barges shuffle silently by and to feel utterly and completely safe walking alone at midnight. I can't do that today. But maybe there is still some hope:

> *Of all the nations in the coalition, I think Hungary has had*
> *a greater thirst for freedom and a greater understanding of*
> *freedom than perhaps any member of the coalition.*

Colin Powell

But where were some of the very best times? Most have been when Athena was with me, such as our 60th birthday celebrations in Hong Kong; collected from the airport in one of the world's best cars and deposited in one of the world's best hotels with a magnificent view over the bustling harbour where, years before, we had leant to sail. And before, on the beaches of the Philippines and Bali and Thailand and sailing together in the seas between Indonesia and Malaysia and between Malaysia and Singapore and around Thailand. Wonderful, exciting and joyous times. But I also loved the songs I sang with my friend Albert as the dawn began to insinuate its presence over the clubs in Taiwan and thus suggested it was time to get back to the hotel for a shower and change before we began another business day together.

> *Taiwan is a part of China's territory and it has never been*
> *a country. There is only one China in the world, and China's*
> *sovereignty and territorial integrity brook no division.*

Wang Guangya – Oh dear, poor Wang, try telling that to the Taiwanese; there is a real world outside China for you to discover, Wang.

The real world that Ferdinand and Imelda Marcos defined and made their own, very successfully for so many years, as dear devious Imelda admitted:

> *We practically own everything in the Philippines.*

126

I loved the time when, alone in a canoe, I paddled lethargically downstream a gorgeous river in Belize. Totally alone as I sang, nay shouted unmelodically, the songs of Billy Fury ('A thousand stars in the sky' – it was shimmering daylight), Elvis's 'It's Now or Never', and a whole bunch of others. And nobody, but no-one could complain, could tell me I was out of tune. The river loved it; the canoe swooned in delight and the steep river banks applauded in wonder. And I loved it. But Belize was a very odd, historically displaced place, as Peter Weir observed:

On one of the surveys for `The Mosquito Coast,' which had stalled, I was in Belize waiting to go across a river, and there was a punt coming toward us, the very punt we would take across the river, ... I thought they were coming back from a fancy dress party, but it was too early in the morning. Then someone told me they were Amish! They got off the punt looking like they were in makeup and wardrobe from an 18th Century production. That was a tremendous hook for me.

Most of my extreme happiness has been in Asia, where I have lived since 1980. The thirty-four years prior to that time were not unpleasant; there were great times also then; but they did not have Athena in them and they did not have Asia in them. I was growing and finding my way and developing my abilities. It was only when I came to Asia that I really felt, I truly felt, I had come home. Unquestionably I knew I had come 'home'. And then I found Athena, and my life was complete. Well, almost complete, I still have much to do. In Asia, as Bai Ling observes with a clarity of understanding of the natural openness and sensuality of most of the Asian races, but not his own:

I was in Asia and people asked me about being considered a sex symbol. I don't know if that's good or not, because where I come from, sex isn't something you're allowed to talk about

But never, ever make the mistake of attempting to move thought processes along too quickly in Asia; as Rudyard Kipling, a man with some experience in Asia, especially India, captured in verse:

127

At the end of the fight is a tombstone white
With the name of the late deceased.
And the epitaph drear, 'A fool lies here
Who tried to hustle the East

XV

Apropos nothing, as I write this I am lying in bed in Chicago, nursing a splitting headache and sinus attack, watching the television and wondering where CNN hold their annual recruitment competition to find the ugliest female newsreaders and weather forecasters in America. They continue to excel in this category, year after year.

Wisdom and age, to what extent do they really go together? Is wisdom in age nothing really more than having had a number of unfortunate experiences and not wishing to repeat them and thus being sufficiently (and boringly) cautious? Is that wisdom?

> *'You are wise'*
> *'No, that is the great fallacy; the wisdom of old men.*
> *They do not grow wise. They grow careful'*
> *'Perhaps that is wisdom'*
> *'It is very unattractive wisdom'*

From 'A Farewell to Arms', by Ernest Hemingway.

Churchill was wiser still when he said:

> *My views are an harmonious process which keeps them*
> *in relation to the current movement of events.*

I think wisdom is acumen, good judgement in difficult situations, perceptiveness and a well-developed insight coupled with more than the average level of intelligence (whatever that is). So who or what can I remember in my life that I could regard as a fine example of wisdom?

Thoreau?

> *If a man does not keep pace with his companions,*
> *perhaps it is because he hears a different drummer.*
> *Let him step to the music he hears,*
> *however measured or far away.*

What about Jules Renard, at the ripe old age of forty in 1904:

> *We don't understand life any better at forty than*
> *at twenty, but we know it and admit it.*

I rather subscribe to a view propounded by William Blake in 'Jerusalem', when he suggested:

> *He who would do good to another, must do it in minute particulars,*
> *general good is the plea of the scoundrel, hypocrite and flatterer*

His wisdom is to suggest that specificity in goodness, (and I also read here, unheralded, unselfish and probably unknown to others), is the only form of real integrity. Maybe best put by Patricia Cornwell in one of her block-buster novels, 'Cruel and Unusual' when discussing an act of charity:

Charity – an act or feeling of goodwill, giving alms to the needy. Charity is giving to someone what he needs versus what you want to give him

But what can we learn from EM Forster, who taking us in 'A Passage to India' along unfamiliar highways and byways and unforgettable people, larger and even sometimes much smaller than life, when he advised:

> *One can tip too much as well as too little, indeed the coin*
> *that buys the exact truth has not yet been minted.*

For ten years I travelled monthly from Hong Kong to Taiwan on business and there met with my business partner, Albert Chen. Now Albert was (and still is at a little over 60) a great singer, drinker, womanizer and philosopher, and an utterly, utterly charming gentleman. He once, in the early hours, following a wicked night, reminded me:

> *Howard, my friend, happiness doesn't mean to increase what you own, but to decrease what you desire.*

That's wisdom, - from at that time, a forty five year-old. Age and wisdom correlation? I don't know. He might also have added a further word of insight, that I recently found in a simple novel by Robert Goddard called, 'Never go back', about a reunion of national servicemen, fifty years after they first served in Scotland. A canny Scot met during the hiatus of the reunion reminded them and indeed, all of us that:

> *Money, money, money. You have to chase it to keep it. And then where's the time for contemplation?*

In business life especially, but perhaps elsewhere in our day-to-day existence, it is always worth considering:

> *Just think what we could achieve if no-one worries who gets the credit.*

I feel that I created that phrase myself some years ago, but I may have read it or heard it somewhere. I'm sorry if I should rather be attributing it to you than to me and I withdraw if you are right.

Evelyn Waugh, in 1963, was charmingly and disarmingly accurate when he pointed out that:

> *Old people are more interesting than young. One of the particular points of interest is to observe how after fifty they revert to the habits, mannerisms and opinions of their parents, however wild they were in youth.*

True? – Are you (assuming you're over fifty or close to) becoming more like your Mum or your Dad in their thoughts, their mannerisms, even the way they used to express themselves, even in their voice inflections, and especially in their lack of patience? In some ways I feel I am, in others, much less so. But maybe it's our mannerisms and hobbies that differ, simply because we have different, often much more, choice available to us than ever they had. They had a war and deprivation and rationing and no TV and no Ipods and no computers and few cars; at least when they were 'growing up'. When did they first travel on a commercial areoplane? First go on an overseas holiday? My father probably when he was forty or fifty. Me when I was twenty five, my children when they were four or five, their children, immediately. What's left? But these are the external trappings; they don't get to the soul of the matter. In extremis, in anger, in love, in public, are you behaving more like your parents than you would care to acknowledge? The genes, the DNA controls are kicking in, no matter what the external forces may be. I think so, I believe so. Did our parents feel as we feel when they reached sixty?

The tragedy of old age is not that one is old, but that one is young.

Oscar Wilde

It's true, I do feel young. I talk with my children and their friends and I <u>really</u> don't feel much older than they are. I wonder what they think of me.

Within I do not find wrinkles and used heart, but unspent youth

Ralph Waldo Emerson.

Or, from William Feather:

Setting a good example for your children
takes all the fun out of middle age

But I truly don't believe I can be accused of that misdemeanor; ask any of my four kids.

132

I do, however, believe most strongly that the man or woman who displays constant enthusiasm for all they do, those that are relentlessly optimistic and cheerful, become almost timeless;

Age may wrinkle the face but lack of enthusiasm wrinkles the soul

I don't know who said this or indeed that which follows, but I may find out before my book is ended; however, the profundidity is absolute:

Every man is enthusiastic at times. One man has enthusiasm for thirty minutes, another man has it for thirty days. But it is the man who has it for thirty years that makes a successful life.

However, it is sadly true to know that, as George Orwell knew:

Not to expose your true feelings to an adult seems to be instinctive from the age of seven or eight onwards.

Did you know that George Orwell, best known for his anti fascist and anti communist novels, 'Animal Farm' and '1984', was born Eric Arthur Blair in 1903? I don't think he was any relation to you know who. He lived only until 1950 (another good one dying far too young).

Let us delve with David Riesman into the development of man. In that progress why and when do most of us lose the opportunity to ripen to our true potential, our greater individuality, our own unique wisdom? If what he says is true, then it is such a shame:

The idea that men are created free and equal is both true and misleading: men are created different: they lose their social freedom and their individual autonomy in seeking to become like each other

When you analyse your life and take stock – at around the age of 60 – you might ask yourself, 'Who am I? What have I achieved? What have I contributed? Brian Mayfield-Smith in his autobiography 'The Outsider – A Personal Journey' has this to recommend:

Two things that have always been important to me in my life have been my independence and my ability to move on. To me these characteristics are at the heart of what life is about, giving us the ability to break the chains of the same old bloody humdrum things. We all go through similar daily processes, forcing ourselves to go forward, convincing ourselves how good things are, when in reality very often we're just plonking along, with nothing to lift us above the daily grind.

I've been exceedingly lucky in most of my endeavours and, as with so many other people, some worked out better than others. On the whole my life has been, thus far, a major positive, at least to me, and were I to be taken tomorrow, I cannot complain.

I've…

- Loved a wonderful woman
- Travelled most of the world
- Written a few books
- Had great children
- Acted, produced and directed some heavy and some lighter drama, and never been ashamed of anything I did on the stage; well, almost never. There was one night when I unbelievably froze on the lines of 'All the World's a Stage', - every schoolboy knows that speech, front back and sideways, yet I froze in mid sentence and adlibbed for two minutes. You just can't adlib that speech, it's akin to adlibbing 'To be or not to be' as 50% of the audience can mouth it, word for word, along with you! Dreadful experience; but set against all the other dramatic positives of my life, forget it; you cannot go back.
- Been a businessman, both as an employee of nationals, multinationals and owning my own companies; the latter on three separate occasions, unfortunately never making much money in any of the three; maybe I am meant to serve rather than to lead? But each experience taught me a lot and I enjoyed every moment
- Been a scholar and managed a couple of degrees, - after the rather limp beginning to my university life when I was in my impressionable low work ethic teens and early twenties

- Sailed my own yacht (with the trusty helmswoman, Athena) across many of the seas of Asia
- Made and lost a million dollars
- Been the editor of two glossy coffee table magazines
- Been a (small scale) property developer – and the houses are still standing!
- Been the only Western CEO of a 100% Korean owned group of companies, in Korea; (freezing cold weather and hot Kimchi)

But… I've never:
- Been proficient in languages other than French and English
- Played a musical instrument beyond an elementary stage
- Painted or drawn anything worth a damn
- Been to Antarctica or the Galapagos islands
- Become consistently moderate in alcohol consumption
- Dedicated myself sufficiently to maintaining personal fitness
- Lived on an animal reserve in Africa
- Achieved a decent golf handicap
- Written a best seller

So now you know some of my life objectives for the next ten years!

But maybe we're getting too heavy, too philosophical; after all, we all rather support D H Lawrence's wise view:

Life is something to be spent, not to be saved.

And I rather like the quotation that I heard (or read) a while ago, but sadly cannot remember who or where, so I cannot attribute it. However, it is:

I'm living so far beyond my means, it could be said that we're living apart

But he or she was obviously a soul mate to William Feather who wisely knew, what most of us know but have never admitted:

A budget tells us what we can't afford, but
it doesn't keep us from buying it

A final word of 'wisdom' in life perhaps, again from William Feather:

Nothing will ruin an interesting intelligent argument
more quickly than the arrival of a pretty girl.

Maybe not final, maybe the last word, as always, should go to the women:

The average girl would rather have beauty than brains because she
knows the average man can see much better than he can think

XVI

History is always good for a giggle, especially when associated with genitals:

As we watch Sears put his genitals into his trousers it is worth observing the look on his face. Sears was a thoughtful man and there was no effrontery or arrogance here, but he seemed to enjoy something very like authority, as if this most commonplace organ, possessed by absolutely every other man on the planet, were some singular treasure, such as the pen that was used for signing the Treaty of Versailles, robbing Bulgaria of Macedonia, giving her Aegean coast to Greece, creating several new quarrelsome nations in the Balkans, expatriating and leaving homeless large populations, giving Poland a corridor to the Baltic and sowing the seeds for future discord and war. Putting his genitals into his trousers, Sear seemed to think he was handling history.

John Cheever

G.M. Young, an historian of some note, is quoted as sounding a lament for the vanished Victorian clerisy (as described in the book 'Victorian People and Ideas' by Richard D. Attick):

And where shall we look for the successors of the Mills and Ruskins and Tennysons? Or of the public for which they wrote? The common residual intelligence is becoming impoverished for the benefit of the specialist, the technician, and the aesthete; we leave behind us the world of historical ironmasters and banker historians, geological divines and

scholar tobacconists, with its genial watchword: to know something of
everything and everything of something: and through the gateway of
the Competitive Examination (for the Civil service, which helped turn
the universities into institutions for specialized professional training)
we go out into the Waste Land of Experts, each knowing so much about
so little that he can neither be contradicted nor is worth contradicting.

When did you last have a wide-ranging conversation with friends over the dinner table; talking of literature and art, of politics and music and history? It's difficult to accomplish this today, most people have such limited knowledge outside their chosen sphere; we have become impoverished through specialization.
The ultimate must surely be to know something of everything and everything of something; otherwise we waste our time on this earth, don't we?

Who said; it sounds to me rather like Churchill,

History is governed by Geography

An old man, speaking to St. Augustine, who was himself an old man, (old being a relative term in those times), had an interesting perspective on history and time:

Time comes from the future, which does not yet exist, into the present
which has no duration, and goes into the past, which has ceased to exist

What is the true barometer of history? Perhaps, as Hendrik Willem Van Loon advised:

The arts are an even better barometer of what is happening in
our world than the stock market or the debates in Congress

I don't think there's much doubt about that, Loony. Indeed, in this context we may also add that:

All progress is made by unreasonable men

Because, if we are all reasonable then we would comply with the norm and forever we'd be viewing plump naked cherubs flouting bows and arrows and possessing small penises and even smaller balls, smiling benignly at the world. But what about that awful painting 'The Cry' by Edvard Munch (sometimes called 'The Scream')? That could never have been created in a world of only cherubs and cherubims, of Madonnas and Constable's (all excellent yet all somewhat boring) fields and ox-carts. The Impressionists were unreasonable, so were the Modernists, so was Elvis and the Beatles and The Rolling Stones and Punk Rock (Ugh!) and Heavy Metal (Ugh, ugh!) – but somehow they all took us forward in creativity and they added rather than took away, because whatever we had, we still have, and whatever they added, we selectively still have and so the circle goes on and becomes ever larger and the sum knowledge, experience enjoyment and history of this delightful and sometimes sordid human race goes on and on, and sometimes, bloody on!

It was George Bernard Shaw, playwright and philosopher, but hardly the greatest of raconteurs or companions, who came up with my previous quote; in full, he said:

> *The reasonable man tries to fit in with the status quo and existing norms. The unreasonable man reacts against the status quo. It therefore follows that all progress is made by unreasonable men.*

I buy it.

How do you tell the youth of today that so many of their 'essential' gadgets, especially their mobile phones, can be unreasonable? One of Robert Goddard's hosts of characters in his mostly readable novels sums it up for me:

> *I hate mobiles. I hate the false urgency they confer on mind-numbingly insignificant exchanges*

Rock on!

Talking of unreasonableness; would anyone of us, if truth be told, want the Islamic faith to have come into this world? But then, without it would we be the poorer? Indeed, would any of us, knowing what we now know, have wanted any religions at all to have graced our world with their terrorism and horror, with their hatred cloaked in bogus love, with their demands and their hypocrisy? If the religions hadn't come, I suppose mankind would have had to, from necessity, create something else; for most people need, even desperately require, something outside themselves, cleverer and superior and better than themselves to cling to so that there can be some real meaning to their lives and they can begin to answer the question, 'what is it all about?' – There are some people that don't need these crutches, I feel I am one of them and thus very lucky, but I may also be bigoted and insecure in other ways that religion could, if I allowed it, make me a little more secure, a little more holy, a little more, - oh, shit, - pleasant and understanding?

However, perhaps the most unreasonable event in history was, as fellow actress Jo's (damn, can't remember her last name, - but she played an excellent Maria to my Toby Belch in Twelfth Night) Dad proclaimed, completely soberly and utterly seriously as we debated late into one Cypriot night:

> *How is it that God, in his infinite wisdom,*
> *ever gave France to the French?*

Just think what improvements could have been made to History if we'd had it!
Just remembered – Taylor.

XVII

But you know, one of the most rewarding activities of well-travelled 60 year olds is the fun to be had in slagging off cultures, nationalities and creeds that have the great misfortune to not have been fashioned after our own. My particular targets over the years have (of course, for an Englishman) been the French, goes without saying; but others such as the grossly rude and un-sweet smelling Chinese can be pretty loathsome, as can, of course the Japanese and Americans en-masse and the impatient unfriendly arrogant Israelis. On the other hand, would you rather have an English beer-reeking low class lout? Gosh!

But some epithet that I am still hoping to discover, maybe invent, has to be reserved for the ugliest of all races, other than most stinkingly grubby Arabs, and that is the almost indescribably gross Russian tourists (in ones or twos they can be great, of course), who Morley Safer captures with consummate clarity in his book 'Flashbacks – on returning to Vietnam':

As for the Russians, not a single one, male or female, weighs in under two hundred forty pounds. Each face is beet red, the Russian skin does not take to tanning. Not a smile graces the lips of even one of them. The women are wearing house dresses, enormous floral sacks that, on these lumpy damp bodies, become form-fitting. Each woman is clutching a handbag of black imitation leather and carrying a shopping bag filled with a dais, *the double slit full length dress and pantaloons that traditional-minded women in Vietnam still wear. Imagine the fashion*

show on some Saturday-night-to-come in Omsk or Novosibirsk. I can
only think of Queen Celeste, wife of Barbar, king of the elephants,
togging up for a tea party, forgoing her normal pink polka dot for one
of these oriental numbers. The Russians grow large in a way that seems
totally different from other nationalities. There is no soft roundness to
them; it is more like layer upon layer of armour-plated elephant hide.

I fear that Morley was not just describing the way they look, but also
their....

Have you ever been to India? What a country of vastness and enormous
contrasts; acute poverty, extreme richness; philosophical debate at
every level, extensive dishonesty and balmy friendships; inspired
entreprenurism and extensive crippling bureaucracy. And appalling
drivers. Why do so many Indian drivers have a death wish?

'Let's see who is the most chicken; I've got the biggest truck. It's of no
matter that the brakes don't work very well and three tyres are bald and
the exhaust seems like an Iraqi oilwell that's just been set alight; I'm
going for it, just watch me, middle of the road, they'll move over.'......
'Oh, golly gosh, oh dear me, they didn't. Oh dear me, oh dear me, I think
they're dead, better get out of here quickly and home to wife and children.'

How does one reconcile this with the gentleness and pacifism, beloved
by Indians and persuasively displayed by that terribly overrated and
smelly little man who changed the face and the potency and the
pretensions of Asia for ever:

Let my house not be walled on four sides
Let all the windows be open,
Let all the cultures blow in
But let no culture blow me off my feet

Mahatma Gandhi

I believe Gandhi was a unpardonable fraud. I don't know but I
would guess that he was justifiably loathed by Churchill, but perhaps
appreciated by Mark Twain, who believed:

India is the cradle of the human race, the birthplace of human speech,
the mother of history, the grandmother of legend, and the great
grandmother of tradition. Our most valuable and most instructive
materials in the history of man are treasured up in India only

Do you know where you belong, where you really belong?

At first I belonged in The Potteries, where great footballers and great writers and punk singers with aspirations to become crooners come from. Stanley Matthews and Arnold Bennett and Robbie Williams. - God preserve us from second class impressionists. Robbie Williams has been reported as being second only to Gerard Depardieu as the world's most rotund sex symbol. Robbie is the archetypal local boy made good. Because of his preferred football allegiance to Port Vale, he isn't really as popular in his home city Stoke, as he should be. Still, he's having a good time, bonking his way around the globe and hopefully keeping other excesses in some form of check. But who cares? I've never enjoyed impersonators.

On the other hand, Arnold Bennett did us proud. He immortalised himself and his city with his descriptive books that may now be a little dated but still retain a literary richness worth the effort of keeping their company for a night or two. He is known for such noble works as 'Anna of the Five Towns', 'Clayhanger' and 'The Card' (also known as 'Denry the Audacious') which told of life in The Potteries. No one knows for sure why Bennett chose to write about 'five towns' when it is six that make up The Potteries, and theories range from 'five' sounding more aesthetically pleasing than 'six' and Fenton (the omitted town) being the home of his mother-in-law!

So, in my formative years, The Potteries was where I believed I belonged, together with the incredibly stalwart and sensitive Josiah Wedgwood who, a little before my time, showed the world how to make real China, how to create prophetic images in clay and was the person who industrialized the manufacture of pottery. He was born in Burslem, one of the 'six' towns in July 1730 and lived only until 1795. He was a member of the Darwin-Wedgwood family, most famously including his grandson, Charles Darwin. Wedgwood married Sarah Wedgwood, a third cousin. Together, they had seven children, the eldest being Susannah Wedgwood who married Robert Darwin and was mother to the English naturalist Charles Darwin. Famous roots making even more famous roots. How often this has happened in history.

We have seen many sons and daughters of The Potteries made good in addition to the above; a couple that you may be more familiar with are Frank Bough, who seems to have been the established TV presenter of all time and John Wain, poet, critic and scholar, whose works, I fear, are little read today.

A tough place, Stoke-on-Trent, hard-hitting, unrelenting, dirty and rough; but not as harsh as the streets of Glasgow where my mother grew up or perhaps even if compared to the struggle of Middlesborough in the nineteen thirties where my father, in a household of women, became the chosen one, the cosseted one, the one that must produce because the others were women and couldn't, weren't allowed, to shine. How my father physically survived, I'll never know, on raisins and nuts and tomato soup and bread, no butter, through his first two years of university because there was bugger all else for the brave new world that was emerging from the stink of the Second World War. But thank God for Churchill, for without him we would now all be Germans and what could be worse than being a German? Well, French perhaps, or maybe American, I suppose; certainly Chinese and indisputably Russian. So, maybe, if Hitler had won, then it wouldn't have been too bad; except for the, you know who's. But still, thank God for Churchill.

He was voted, in the year 2000, as the greatest Englishman who had ever lived; knocking Shakespeare and Nelson and Maggie Thatcher (was she was a man after all?) into the proverbial cocked hat. But when he was also voted the greatest personality of the 20th Century, all of Mohammed Ali's (ex Cassius Clay – remember?) fans took umbrage and were up in fists, - little good it did them though. Poor Ali, what a superman he truly was at his absolute best and to be reduced by Parkinson's disease to what he is today; and you still believe in God?

Sing on, let the music play...

Music, well, what can one say about music that has not been said before except to articulate that it is the greatest leveller of all time, greater than art, than sex, than food or wine, greater than the spoken or written word. Why is music so absolute? Because listening is all that is required; all that is called for and anyone, anywhere can listen. The man in the cell, the HIV patient dying in the bed, the lovers on the edge of ecstasy, the bereaved in their greatest moment of loss, the young brave on his first adventure in life, to kill, to mount, to overcome. There is simply and irrevocably, nothing in this world as powerful as music. Just nothing. It is often like coming home to a blanket of security and love.

> *Some men (and women) are born out of their due place. Accident has cast them amid certain surroundings, but they always have nostalgia for a house they know not.... Perhaps it is this sense of strangeness that sends men far and wide in search of something permanent to which they may attach themselves.... Sometimes a man hits upon a place to which he mysteriously feels that he belongs. Here is the home he sought, and he will settle amid scenes that he has never seen before, among men he has never known, as though they were familiar to him from his birth*

Thus Somerset Maugham, in 1959, put into words exactly what I felt on my first visit to Asia in 1980, as I drove from the gloriously exciting old Hong Kong airport downtown to take up my new job.

And so to Vietnam; why? Well, what do we really know about this sadly desecrated, proud and pitiless country?

What a terrible mistake was the war in Vietnam; for everyone; for both sides. No-one had learnt anything from history; no-one continues to learn, even today. The arrogance of the Americans met the intransigence of the Vietnamese. And still it is today. Why the hell can't the Americans and even most of the Europeans and even the sad English, read and understand history, especially as they made most of it? Does America really believe it can ever have influence over the oriental mind? A mind and a culture Aeons ancient even before

America ever came into existence. Oh dear me, they really can't get it can they?

> *The Vietnamese have close to fifty thousand troops in*
> *a country where the gross national product is nothing*
> *more than two million orgasms a month*

Stirling Silliphant – Silver Star

But those orgasms give it the vitality and the innocence and the enthusiasm and the dominance that can never be defeated by a soft underbelly state such as America. And yet, and yet, they just don't get it. The Americans, I mean. And even we British can't get through to them, perhaps it is as Churchill once remarked:

> *Two peoples, the American and the English,*
> *separated by a common language*

Maybe we are being a little unfair to our erstwhile colony, Albert Einstein understood many things better than most and he particularly understood what compels most Americans:

> *The American lives even more for his goals, for the future, than*
> *the European. Life for him is always becoming, never being*

That truly does capture a lot for us to think about. It encapsulates, in one sentence why it is that the Americans will never understand the Asians, or indeed vice-versa. For most Asians live for the here and now, feeling that they have little or no control over their fate; often believing that they are where they are because of what they did, good or bad, in a previous life. They certainly believe they have little influence on their future, so much, they often think, is preordained.

How can tomorrow talk with today?

Consider how emotions are released or kept in check, dependant upon culture. Arabs rhythmically beat their breasts and wail at funerals, Europeans sob and cry, sometimes ashamedly, sometimes openly:

I have very rarely seen anybody cry at a funeral in Thailand and I have never once seen the sort of hysterics that are common at funerals in the West. I think this pragmatic attitude shows a very profound understanding of the Buddha's teaching about the impermanent nature of all things. At the same time, perhaps this understanding is also at least partly responsible for the Thai's ability to enjoy themselves on a moment-to-moment basis, without worrying too much about what the future might hold. There is only one certainty in this life and that is that it ends.

From 'Phra Farang', - 'An English Monk in Thailand', by Peter S. Robinson

Do all Buddhists everywhere behave as the Thais do at funerals? Is it a cultural thing or a religious thing? What an interesting study for someone to make; do emotional displays stem culturally or religiously?

XVIII

How many of us have been blessed with finding, enjoying and basking in true love? I have. And I am so grateful that I know what it is. And I also know that with love there is hope for mankind. Segal said it better:

> *The imperfections of the human state are*
> *outweighed by the glory of human love*

What is it, this thing called love?

Kenneth Clark, in his autobiography, 'Another part of the wood', expressed, often by innuendo, his constant and abiding love for his wife, but, as I believe he would readily admit, love can often be blind. He recounts:

> *At the time I was courting Jane, the only present I gave her was a paper bag of peppermint bullseyes. In Venice* (on honeymoon) *the weather was warm, and Jane had brought only one thin dress. She wore it for a fortnight, as she thought it would be rude to ask me to buy her another, and of course it never occurred to me to do so.*

Again, I might ask; what is it, this thing called love? Is it really blind?

Love has many features, many elements, many faces.

Love is, quite simply, giving; being quiet when the other, the one you love, is struggling to express something and you know you know the words better than he or she does, but you remain quiet because he or she has to find them for him/herself and if you give them to him/her you are taking something away, and not giving.

Love is knowing when to stop and when not to try to be superior and love is listening and not talking and not pontificating, even though you know best, and love is giving and never taking and being prepared and consciously becoming second because your love is more important than being first. Love is surrendering all and everything and yet still being yourself and strong, and love is enjoying her music and her friends who, normally you would have no time for, and love is giving her the last glass of champagne in the bottle and forgoing it yourself even though you die for Moet. Love is never criticizing her play on the seventh green, even though you feel she could do better if she listened to you, and love is holding her in the distress that you don't understand or relate to, but that is her real distress and her real relationship that you have never been privy to nor understand but it is of no consequence because she is hurting and that is so much more important than whatever caused the pain you will never understand.

Finally, love is never wanting to go on, for one breath longer than she takes; love is knowing and believing and acting on the fact, the absolute, the irrefutable reality that her first breath and her last breath is also and ever, yours. That's what love is. And I found that love.

Athena.

But I know she hates me for, at least, one thing...

Early morning cheerfulness can be extremely obnoxious

William Feather

I am the most cheerful person in the early morning. Just ask her, before she gets rid of me!

But deep down, it is the strength of the roots that count. An ancient Chinese proverb will put it better than most of us can manage:

As long as the trunk is firm, worry not over
the branches swaying in the wind

As I write this section of my little book it's November 2006 and I've just spent five hours cycling along the sun drenched but chilly banks of the Han River that bisects the great city of Seoul. And I made a life decision. I hope I shall have the courage to carry it out, if sadly I am called upon to do so.

I have decided that I will not outlive my wife. I just feel that there is really no point to my life is she is taken from me prematurely; absolutely no point whatsoever.
Some people live for their children, some for their grandchildren, some, even, for their parents or even their animals. I live for Athena; it's as simple as that.

And it's great!

In a somewhat different context and with rather less intensity, GK Chesterton in 'The Man who was Thursday' describes relationships thus:

There are no words to express the abyss between isolation and
having one ally. It may be conceded to the mathematicians
that four is twice two. But two is not twice one; two is
two thousand times one. That is why, in spite of a hundred
disadvantages, the world will always return to monogamy

The weather on my bike ride was chilly at something less than 10 degrees centigrade, brought down further by a few more degrees because of the wind chill factor. But not a cloud in the Korean sky, rather a gentle blue welcoming light. The sun shining brightly and warming when I found a wind sheltered spot by the river. I had picked a book from my shelf to accompany me on the ride and had turned my Ipod to Elvis's greatest hits. I decided that I'd picked up the wrong – in the sense it did not match my mood – book, 'written lovingly but without fuss' as the dust jacket proclaimed, by John Gunther. A memoir of his brilliant son and that son's death from a brain tumour, at the age of seventeen. The book is called, 'Death be not proud', - I'll get to it at the right moment. Not in the mood now. I should have brought Georgie Best's autobiography, entitled 'Blessed', that could have been more fun, - but maybe that will be his tale of dying from alcoholism; - oh dear.

Another decision I made on my journey was that Elvis is much better to watch and hear than to just listen to; although I have to admit that he remained switched on for the entire five hours, and only repeated two songs in the whole of that time; phenomenal! Johnny Mathis, on the other hand is 's'wonderful, s'wonderful' to hear, but somehow detracts from his own excellence when you watch him. He has the stage presence of a piece of mahogany.

The Han River, mostly wide, occasionally narrow, pulses through the city of Seoul where the city managers have done a terrific job of providing pathways, jogging tracks, roller blading and cycle tracks along the length of this great river; too far along for me to cycle, but there is always tomorrow. The pathways are clean, sometimes decorated with informative pictures of flora and fauna to be found along the route, descriptions written in both Korean and English; music plays at certain points (ugh! – Orwell's 1984 ish) and everything is safe. Children, very young children, walk, play, cycle together; not an adult in sight, none is necessary; no-one would harm the children. Not in Korea. Old granddads walk on the arms of their children and grandchildren, the family unit is so tight, loving and caring in this society; no old people's homes for Koreans. Is that a good thing? – I guess it is when you are old. Sixty is not old, Howard, unless you are infirm or unloved; then it's very very old.

On the other hand, (as every good economist would say – they always must have options), grand old, (he was always old), Bertrand Russell has these wise words to say about love:

*Of all the forms of caution, caution in love is
perhaps the most fatal to true happiness.*

It's funny how difficult it is to see some people, such as Bertrand, in the role of a great lover. And how wrong we can be.

Remember one of the greatest lines from (I think) a Barbara Streisand film? - It goes:

Love is – knowing no-one else will do

If you've never felt this, then I am genuinely sorry for you. I have been blessed with this feeling, this knowledge. It lives with me every day and will continue to do so as long as Athena is with me. And she will always be with me.

There is, however, one quotation I'm still struggling with, that I think I understand, but I'm not quite sure; it possesses such depth and heartrending profundity:

You never realize death until you realize love

Katherine Butler Hathaway

Some people, those who are less sentimental would probably balk at the inclusion of the next anonymous quotation from a 19th Century poet; but, is it less poignant for being relatively unknown? Is its message less vibrant and uplifting today than when it was penned many years ago? I think not, for why else would it have found its way into my little book? I suspect that over the century or more since it was written, this poignant piece has been an inspiration and a source of succor to many:

*Do not stand at my grave and weep,
I am not there, I do not sleep.
I am a thousand winds that blow,
I am the diamond glints in snow.
I am the sunlight on ripened grain,*

152

I am the gentle autumn rain.
When you awaken in the morning's hush
I am the swift uplifting rush
Of quiet birds in circled flight.
I am the soft stars that shine at night.
Do not stand at my grave and cry,
I am not there. I did not die

I promised myself, when I began writing this little book, that I wouldn't over indulge in my favourites, but how, in God's good earth can we exclude Hemingway and his insights? So I surrender to one of my boyhood heroes and one of the shapers of my thoughts, especially about true love and true feeling and I offer you this from 'For Whom the Bell Tolls' – if you haven't read this book, you should be deeply ashamed:

They were walking through the heather of the mountain meadow and Robert Jordan felt the brushing of the heather against his legs, felt the weight of the pistol in its holster against his thigh, felt the sun on his head and on his back and, in his hand, he felt the girl's hand firm and strong. The fingers locked in his. From it, from the palms of her hand against the palms of his, from their fingers locked together, and from her wrist across his wrist something came from her hand, her fingers and her wrist to his that was as fresh as the first light air that moving toward you over the sea barely wrinkles the glassy surface of a calm, as light as a feather moved across one's lips, or a leaf falling when there is no breeze, so light that it could be felt with the touch of their fingers alone, but that was so strengthened, so intensified, and made so urgent, so aching, and so strong by the hard pressure of their fingers and the close pressed palm and wrist, that it was as though a current moved up his arm and filled his whole body with an aching hollowness of wanting. With the sun shining on her hair, tawny as wheat, and on her golden-brown smooth-lovely face, and on the curve of her throat he bent her head back and held her to him and kissed her.

Don't you wish you could have written that? Experienced that? Can you take some more? If you have a soul, if you have ever loved, enjoy some more…

Then there was the smell of heather crushed and the roughness of the bent stalks under her head and the sun bright on her closed eyes and all his life he would remember the curve of her throat with her head pushed back into the heather roots and her lips that moved smally (who else could get away with a word like that?) *and by themselves and the fluttering of the lashes on the eyes tight closed against the sun and against everything, and for her everything was red, orange, gold red from the sun on the closed eyes, and it all was that colour. For him it was a dark passage which led to nowhere, then to nowhere, then again to nowhere, once again to nowhere, always and forever to nowhere, heavy on the elbows in the earth to nowhere,* (the rhythm of love, of lovemaking, of giving and receiving and did you, did you ever experience this?) *dark, never any end to nowhere, now not to be borne once again always and to nowhere, now beyond all bearing up, up, up, and into nowhere, suddenly, scaldingly, holdingly,* (wonderful word invention) *all nowhere gone and time absolutely still and they were both there, time having stopped and he felt the earth move out and away from under them...And the earth moved. The earth never moved before.*

Is there any writer that could ever do better than this to describe the climax of love; the climax of two people joined together as one? How many of us can say we have ever experienced this sublime culmination and can even begin to attempt to describe it? How many of us have genuinely felt the earth move? I can't even find the words to express my thoughts. I simply cannot follow Hemingway.......
Later, maybe...

Let us allow Albert Camus to tidy up our displaced emotions with an undemanding phrase from 'The Outsider':

> *What does eternity to me? To lose the touch of flowers and woman's hands is the supreme separation.*

XIX

Let's ramble for a while, as if we haven't been doing so for ages! Now, about Confucius, does anyone really know anything about him, save what he is credited with chattering on about? For example, what did he mean when he said:

As the water shapes itself to the vessel that contains it,
so a wise man adapts himself to circumstances

Yes, I guess, we do understand, but is it that profound? We spend our life being told how profound the Confucius's of the world are. But, when we analyze the above 'wisdom' then all it says is that 'we adjust ourselves to the circumstances of the moment' – Yes, somewhat obvious really, isn't it? Who needs a sage?

What is a philosopher, anyway? A prophet? What is a prophet? Michael Ffinch tries to help by suggesting:

A prophet is one whose inspired vision of the world enables him to
speak out accurately against the errors of his time. By reminding
his people of past faults and pointing out the follies of the present
he may predict that, if his promptings go unheeded, an inevitably
disastrous future will follow. Thus it is not only through a true
interpretation of the present that a prophet may be said to foretell
the future, and those who came after him are able to see with the
benefit of hindsight whether his prophecy was true or false.

You know, in connection with not much else, but prophetically, E.W. Howe, had something rather poignant to leave us with when he said:

*Some men storm imaginary alps all their lives, and die in
the foothills cursing difficulties which do not exist*

Gautama Buddha probably put the world and the human state into correct perspective when he pessimistically declared:

There is no fire like passion,
There is no shark like hatred,
There is no snare like folly,
There is no torrent like greed.

I understand the imagery, except for the shark. However, moving on...

Are we rambling? Or are we discovering some profound truths about ourselves, about the human race, about our very fears of being here in a life and a lifetime we neither understand nor can come to terms with? Are we rather like Alf Todd (a creation of the, should be, revered, P.G. Wodehouse) who described:

*'Alf Todd,' said Ukridge, soaring to an impressive burst of
imagery, 'has about as much chance as a one-armed blind
man in a dark room trying to shove a pound of melted
butter into a wild cat's left ear with a red hot needle'*

Don't you wish you possessed such an imagination?

But why do some of us have a better chance of shoving the melted butter into a wild cat's left ear than others? Is it ability, luck or chance? I think it's all of these things, but the greatest of them all is persistence. A person who has the persistence, the determination to succeed, the doggedness, despite all the odds to keep on going towards their aim despite failures, despite setbacks, is the one who will get the melted butter into the wild cat's ear.

I've found, over the years, that much as we may hate them, there is little that is more persistent (some say pernicious) than the advertising fraternity of smart and sexy young men and women who simply delight in spending other people's money; quite gratuitously, as if they are benevolently creating works of art. Stephen Leacock understands that world only too well, as he informs us:

Advertising may be described as the science of arresting the human intelligence long enough to get money from it

Was anything said with greater truth? Yet their persistency wins through, every time. They are to be admired rather than castigated. Aren't they?

Charles Dickens was rejected by so many publishers, so many times, despite his persistence, that, in the end, he decided to transform this persistence into creative self-publishing. The rest is a glorious history. Colonel Sanders took his recipe for special fried chicken to almost 1,000 companies over many years before one decided to take a chance on him and Kentucky Fried Chicken hit the streets of the world. Look at Richard Branson, his ups and downs, sheer bloody determination kept him going until he reached the top. Success rarely comes easily, even to the less worthy. The aggressive footballer has, usually, worked hard all his (young) life, the newly discovered actress has been through her own hell and will go through much more to be where she is today and to remain there.

What is the alternative? Mediocrity? Mine, yours. Is it enough for us to simply get by in this competitive world? Sure it is, and it can be a happy state too. But not very satisfying or fame creating!

My daughter, Nicole, once, at a low point in my life, and maybe in hers; as she was just about to sit her 'A' level exams in South Island School in Hong Kong, sent me this:

There are only two things to worry about; either you are sick or OK, - if you're OK, then there's nothing to worry about. If you are sick, then there's only two things to worry about. – Either you live

157

or die. If you live, there's nothing to worry about. If you die then there's only two things to worry about, - either you go to Heaven or to Hell. If you go to Heaven, there's nothing to worry about. If you go to Hell, you'll be so damn busy shaking hands with all your friends you won't have time to worry! So, - why worry?

I remember a similar piece from the same source:

When I look back on all these worries, I remember the story of the old man who said on his deathbed that he had had a lot of trouble in his life, most of which had never happened

Many people, wiser (whatever that is, see previous), than you and I, have attempted to tell us how, where and why to challenge mediocrity, here is Dag Hammarskjold:

We are not permitted to choose the frame of our destiny. But what we put into it is ours

Or the famous 'Anon'

*If it's worth doing
It's worth doing right.
If it's not worth doing right,
It's not worth doing at all.
If it can't be done right,
Do something else right instead*

Or, from the same author:

Everything comes to him who hustles while he waits

Oliver Cromwell, remember him? The guy with the funny (as in peculiar) round hat and even funnier flat personality, did manage to grunt this out:

He who stops being better, stops being good

What ho, Olly! But inside there's an unambiguous truth for all of us. Those of us that do not continue to strive, to better ourselves in knowledge or behaviour, no matter what our age or experience; those of us who become TV addicts or couch potatoes or drink dependants or newspaper wallowers are already lost; we are no longer getting better, thus we are no longer good. For ourselves, for our companions, for our families, for our friends.

He who does not hope to win, has already lost

Jose Joaquin Olmedo

Courage is necessary to achieve more than mediocrity, as George Gissing reminds us

Have the courage of your desire

I think I understand what he means; if you desire something enough, articulate it in some way and determine what you need to do to attain it that you are not doing now and have the courage to do just that; then you will achieve your desire.

But courage is different things to different people; I remember waking up in my hotel room in Russia (the desperately cold one) in the depths of a dark night and seeing two huge hulking figures going through my luggage. Both were as black as the room. I could have had the courage to accost them, I could have had a different kind of courage and closed my eyes and pretended to sleep, hoping they would not accost me before they left. I could have done either.

The highest courage is to dare to appear to be what one is

That from John Lancaster Spalding, - that night I certainly dared to appear to be what I is!
However, I rather subscribe now to the view of Sir Arthur Helps when he astutely recognises:

The sense of danger is never, perhaps, so fully comprehended
as when the danger has been overcome.

I feel that now about those guys in my hotel room, or the Italian customs officer I punched in the face after losing my cool with his unnecessarily officious attitude, or the guy, who briefly, lived next door to me, a real 'shit' (excuse me) of a person, who I frequently became more than verbally aggravated with, only to learn afterwards that he was on America's Most Wanted List of criminals. This, I only found out after he had pulled a gun on one of his ex-wives, the third ex. I think, and she had grabbed it and turned it on him, shot three times and left him dying on the floor of a restaurant in Chiang Mai. It gives me goose pimples to remember what he once said to me when we were in the heat of one of our 'discussions':

'You are a very lucky man, Howard, that I'm
not going to take this further today

I can only imagine he didn't have his gun in his pocket at that precise moment.

Logan Pearsall Smith suggests:

What is more mortifying than to feel that you have missed
the plum for want of courage to shake the tree?

How many plums have I missed in life? How many have you? Desire Joseph Cardinal Mercier, had this to say on the subject:

So few men have the courage to question themselves
in order to ascertain what they are really capable of
becoming. And so few have the will to become it

Interestingly, Henry Ford, never a chaser after fame or fortune, managed to realize both and he achieved them, as he recounted in 1915:

Wealth, like happiness, is never attained when sought after directly.
It always comes as a by-product of providing a useful service.

Is this still correct today? Many would argue not, but analyze the word 'service' – it means to assist, to benefit, to do a good turn, to give an advantage to someone, to help another, to, in a different sense, 'tune-up' someone or something. Do the overpaid sportsmen and women of the world, and the grossly overpaid movie actors and actresses provide a service? Does the arrogantly successful businessman as he climbs uncaringly over the lives and hopes of many, provide a service to many more? – You make your own judgement. If Henry is right, then service equals wealth. Get out and get servicing! Follow James B. Conant's turtle:

Behold the turtle, he makes progress only when his neck is out

However, miracles may sometimes happen, so when they do, please have the good grace, as Harry F. Banks advises:

If at first you succeed, try to hide your astonishment

And, when you don't succeed, when progress eludes you, when defeat looms, remember this from Hemingway, from 'The Old Man and the Sea', before you reach your lowest, lowest ebb:

A man can be destroyed but not defeated

XX

Animals: - that means mainly dogs, at least for my wife and I, who have a couple of delightful, unshowable at Crufts, mongrels; but I'm sure with a little persuasion and enough of my wine, you could come to believe that at least one of them is, almost, a thoroughbred Beagle, well, pretty close; with amazing Queen Anne legs; God, Anne must have walked funny with legs like that!

For our sins and pleasures, Athena and I have been Operations Director and Chairman, in that order, of the Phuket Animal Welfare Society, getting on for ten years now. The only active Animal Welfare Society in the Southern part of Thailand that looks after, cares for, sterilizes and manages the stray dog and cat population, of which there are thousands. We have been called upon to help with bears, elephants, monkeys, horses, eagles, owls, storks and hornbills, but dogs and cats are our daily fare. We survive purely on donations from kind hearted locals and tourists and what we are able to put in ourselves, which is mainly hours, especially from the (over) committed Athena. Most proceeds from this little book, whenever it goes into profit, will be channeled to this charity. Why?

Animals are such agreeable friends – they ask
no questions, they pass no criticisms

George Eliot

In any one year we sterilize at least six thousand animals using our mobile field clinic and our static clinic at headquarters. Now, if you reckon that in each litter there are just 4 babies, often there are many more, then we have saved the streets, temples, highways and beaches of Phuket from being littered with some 24,000 animals per year, and we have been doing this for ten years now. Do the maths. But still, after all these years, I cannot watch as one of our stunningly gorgeous Thai vets (we have three, each prettier than the next, - why do you think I stay?) removes the balls from a pulsating sack. Ugh! – I can easily watch as a female loses her ovaries, but to take away a chap's balls, - Oh, no can do!

Dogs are cuddly, majestic, independent yet dependent, ask nothing save sustenance and love and return that love tenfold. They are not complicated or moody as children are; they are unwaveringly loyal, never require pocket money or new clothes or material things. And they guard and look after you. Who, in their right mind can possibly prefer children to dogs? I just don't get it.

With their father, the alpha cattle-slayer, dead, it was to their mother that they and the two young adults now looked for leadership. Heedless of the collar on her neck, (a heavy iron collar that had been attached before she had broken away from capture by the trapper who had killed her mate) *it was she alone now who roused them from their lazy afternoon rests and mustered them for the hunt. It was she who led them in sinewed file through the autumn gloam of the forest, who stopped to sniff the cold night air for the waft of prey, who chose which lesser life to spare and which to take*

From 'The Loop', by Nicholas Evans

There is so little we understand about animals and that is because we spend so little time observing and learning from them. In the art of communication, more than 50% is attributed to body language, while less than 10% from words; so observation is key. I recently saw on the BBC news where a totally black shrouded and completely veiled teacher was taking her local authority to court as it was requesting her to remove the veil so that the students could see and hear what she said, and she was refusing. My God! – What total and absolute nonsense this world has become! However, back to the animals, at least there's more sense to be gleaned there.

Robertson Davies strikes to the heart of man and dog relationships when he said:

> *The dog is a yes-animal, very popular with people*
> *who can't afford to keep a yes-man*

Some truth in that, but he never took my dog Oscar for a walk. As I said, it's almost a Beagle and anyone who knows anything at all about this breed will tell you that it's great for following smells and developing a one-track approach in so doing. You try and get it to come to heel once it's had a whiff of something particularly appealing and you'll walk home alone. Totally untrainable. Not much 'yes-man' about Oscar. But does that matter when you constantly realize, as did Josh Billings who graced this world with his wisdom from 1818 to 1885:

A dog is the only thing on earth that loves you more than he loves himself.

Churchill, although keeping dogs himself (well, he had to, didn't he, as the epitome of the British bulldog), sometimes became a little less than loyal to man's best friend. I can only believe that he was suffering from influenza or maybe a surfeit of brandy when he proclaimed:

> *I like pigs. Dogs look up to us. Cats look down*
> *on us. Pigs treat us as equals.*

However, let's dwell for a moment with Ezra Pound, not a man to argue with, especially when he advised us in 'Meditatio':

> *When I carefully consider the curious habits of dogs, I am compelled*
> *to conclude that man is the superior animal. When I consider the*
> *curious habits of man, I confess, my friend, I am puzzled.*

164

I've never really taken much time to understand horses. It may hark back to when I was around 21 years old and I was talked into horse riding by a girl I rather fancied in the office – would you believe I worked for the Inland Revenue at that time – the first job I'd taken after being sent down from university – did I tell you that story? – Another time… Anyway, off on Sunday mornings to Barlaston in Staffordshire, (an hour from where I lived in Chell, Stoke-on-Trent; shades of Arnold Bennett) with my then fiancé and this girl I rather fancied and her husband; all to ride across The Downs. Me for the girl, them for the horses; at least I think so. I had a few Sundays at this nonsense until one day, passing across an icy road from one field to another, my large white stallion slipped on the icy white roadway and down we went. On reflection I was exceedingly lucky for, despite being pinned under his weighty frame, the worst I suffered was no more than a broken finger, but somehow, after that salutary event, I felt a little less of The Lone Ranger than I had hitherto and began to forego such Sunday outings with increasing regularity.

Brian Mayfield-Smith, one of the top Australian horse trainers and an intelligent bruiser with a great love of all animals, had this to say about horses, in his autobiography; 'The Outsider – A Personal Journey':

> *Horses, in one respect at least, are like humans – each of them is different. The thing I have admired most over the years about some of my really 'genuine' horses, is their sincerity. With horses there are no strings attached, no hidden agendas. How different that is from humans, who always seem to have an 'angle' in what they do – whether visible or invisible. A horse doesn't get inspiration from anywhere except within itself. When a horse really puts in, it is from his or her own heart. And that is what I admire most about them – the fact that they haven't got an angle. They are just pure.*

Isn't that the same for all animals? At least it is in my experience.

But he also said:

*I always reckoned there were two things in life that could make
an idiot of you – one of them is women, and the other is horses*

I agree to a point, but I can think of one or two more. Money and
alcohol spring readily to mind; but there are others.

Where do most of us view animals and learn of them? Some of us
are lucky enough to have been on safari and seen them up close, but
only for a short time, often barely for an instant as we are driven
on in the obliging jeep (actually, usually a Toyota Land Cruiser) to
the next viewing point, for the next animal viewing. I love Africa,
I and my wife would live there in an instant to study and enjoy
the animals, but, where to live? Much of that wonderful and sad
continent is in turmoil. We visited Zimbabwe and even met Mugabi,
before he became a wanton lunatic; my wife once had Idi Amin in
her kitchen. Scary. I learned to love and revere the exploits of David
Livingstone when I was a youth; but where to live now? South Africa
is almost completely a gated community, or, rather, a many gated
community. Alright for those comfortable with having guns in their
homes and cars, to pop at the guy who walks menacingly to your
vehicle when the traffic lights have turned red. Guns under your
pillow at night and guards patrolling outside your door. No, not for
me. Zimbabwe today is virtually dead; thank goodness we saw it
when it was vibrant. Mozambique will still take many many years
to recover from its internally inflicted waste and natural flooding
disasters. Kenya seems to be on the way out; the herds are depleted,
the tourism traps are squalidly laying waste to the land. Can you
imagine when the Russians and the Chinese 'discover' cheap travel
in Africa? It will simply disappear under the weight of insensitive
mediocrity and sink.

But back to where most people, especially young impressionable
minds, meet animals. The zoo! And here's an interesting viewpoint
concerning zoos, from Yann Martel, in his novel, 'The Life of Pi':

*I have heard nearly as much nonsense about zoos as I have about God
and religion. Well-meaning but misinformed people think animals in
the wild are 'happy' because they are 'free'. They imagine this wild*

166

animal roaming about the savannah on digestive walks after eating a prey that accepted its lot piously, or going for callisthenic runs to stay slim after overindulging. Being denied its 'freedom' for too long, the animal becomes a shadow of itself, its spirit broken. So some people imagine. This is not the way it is. Animals in the wild lead lives of compulsion and necessity within an unforgiving social hierarchy in an environment where the supply of fear is high and the supply of food low, and where territory must constantly be defended and parasites forever endured. What is the meaning of freedom in such a context? Animals in the wild are, in practice, free neither in space nor in time, nor in their personal relations In the wild, animals stick to the same paths for the same pressing reasons, season after season. In a zoo, if an animal is not in its normal place in its regular posture at the usual hour, it means something....Don't we say, 'There's no place like home?' That's certainly what animals feel. Animals are territorial. That is the key to their minds. Only a familiar territory will allow them to fulfill the two relentless imperatives of the wild: the avoidance of enemies and the getting of food and water. A biologically sound zoo enclosure — whether cage, pit, moated island, corral, terrarium, aviary or aquarium — is just another territory. Finding there is no need to go hunting, the animal happily claims and protects its space.

Interesting, certainly thought stimulating.

However, there is no question but that David Attenborough should be prescribed viewing for all schools everywhere, at least five hours per week; then there may be some hope for our planet. Instead, the kids are given a diet of computer literacy and algebra. Bye, bye....

XXI

Who are the great leaders; not just great, but also good? Despite everything, it can be argued that, for many, Hitler was a great leader and so too Castro and Mussolini and Gadaffi and Mao and even Nixon. But were they 'good'?

One maxim of President Dwight D. Eisenhower that he practiced and preached when he was the general leading the Allied forces in Europe during the Second World War was as follows. He would frequently demonstrate the veracity of his words by deploying a simple piece of string; he would put it on a table and say:

'Pull it and it will follow wherever you go.
Push it and it will go nowhere'

I have used his phrase countless times in my business life, coaching others, especially new managers, as to what is expected of them. It invariably impresses. I hope they remember to apply the maxim. I'm certain many so called leaders that I've met, don't!

John Howard, who few could have imagined as a great leader or statesman, possesses an unassuming style bundled together with sound constant commonsense that has ensured his longevity as a Prime Minister, much longer than many other so called charismatic leaders. After ten years as Prime Minister of Australia in 2006 and having won four elections he was interviewed by a journalist who asked the question, 'Where does your stamina come from?' John Howard's reply:

> *I've fortunately got a strong constitution, so that's a great help. I'm disciplined, I exercise. One of the secrets of high-pressure jobs, whether in politics or business, is eating regularly. I never miss meals. Never. The number of people I come across who say, 'I didn't have time for lunch'. Well, that's nonsense. It doesn't matter who you are, you've got time for lunch.*

Remember that comment when someone is attempting to impress you with his industriousness during the lunch hour. In, at least John Howard's opinion, he's probably incapable of managing anything if he can't manage time to take lunch.

XXII

The artist is the creator of beautiful things.
To reveal art and conceal the artist is art's aim

So said Oscar. It's not difficult to follow his thought, but Albert Camus is a little more challenging when he suggests:

Without freedom, no art;
Art lives only on the restraints it imposes on itself, and dies of all others

Perhaps, read it again and all will be clear.

We all have our artistic favourites and our horrors. I used to enjoy the works of John Constable, (1776-1837) but not any more. I guess I moved on.

Constable's painting of the Hay Wain, perhaps his most famous work, was exhibited at the Royal Academy in 1821, the year it was painted, but failed to find a buyer. Yet when exhibited in France, with other paintings by Constable, the artist was awarded a gold medal by Charles X. – I don't think I'd have bought it or even given it a gold medal, but others still love it, even today. Why? Did he achieve what Oscar Wilde was looking for in art, revealing art and concealing the artist? I don't think so. But I feel differently about The Impressionists.

I never cared for The Impressionists, until my daughter Nicole bought me a book of their paintings when I was studying for my Open University degree (during my first early retirement in Cyprus). This fresh swirly colourful and vivid world entered my home and my mind. Fat squashed people drinking lots of wine and eating cheese in absurd positions of splendid lethargy or crazy trees emerging from crazier flowers and brilliant swathes of colour romping through fields and minds and, oh, such completely superb nonsense. Well done Manet and Pissarro, Degas and Monet, Renoir and Van Gogh, Gauguin and Cezanne – all good old English names!

Manet spoke for them all when he said:

I paint what I see, not what others like to see

Then he went ahead (in 1863) and did just that by producing the most unutterably silly painting, named 'Luncheon on the Grass', where he displayed two bewhiskered gents, sitting fully garbed in morning coats, shirts and ties, apparently deep in philosophical conversation whilst, beside them, posingly provocatively, reclines a voluptuously naked and astonishingly well-endowed pure white-skinned lady; another of her evident sex, similarly unattired, paddles some little distance away in the stream. The gentlemen continue to speak of wisdom and existence, apparently blissfully unaware of the startling reality of life so manifestly displayed before them. What totally silly nonsense. 'I paint what I see', he said. Wish I had his eyes!

But art is not always wonderful rompings through delightful emotions. The image of that grim work, 'The Scream', as mentioned before, sometimes called 'The Cry' by the gifted Norwegian painter and printmaker, Edvard Munch, who was not only his country's greatest artist, but also played a vital role in the development of German expressionism, will forever remain in my soul and that of many others, and I really can't explain why.

His work often included the symbolic portrayal of such themes as misery, sickness and death. What has happened in the life of someone to have to create such an anguished expression of isolation and fear?

I shudder to think and thank, whoever there may be to thank, that whatever I have thus far experienced in my life does not come close to the anguish he portrays. Maybe one day, or, rather, inevitably one day, - for all of us.

See what that picture does!

He knows all about art, but he doesn't know what he likes.

James Thurber (1894 - 1961)

Ezra Pound, who was not always the easiest person to follow in argument or to comprehend exactly his messages, had this to say in 1954 (he lived from 1885-1973 so he had a fair crack at understanding some things) about images in art; it needs (at least for me) to be read a couple of times to understand what he's getting at:

> *An 'image' is that which presents an intellectual and emotional complex in an instant of time...It is the presentation of such a 'complex' instantaneously which gives that sense of sudden liberation; that sense of freedom from time limits and space limits; that sense of sudden growth, which we experience in the presence of the greatest works of art.*

We should constantly keep an open mind as to what constitutes art. And that from me! One who has been noticeably closed to a number of new ideas, as indeed we all are. Sadly as we become older, it would seem that the gates become narrower; nonetheless, we should strive to keep them as wide as possible for as long as possible. So what is art? Is a peepshow art? I think what immediately follows is art, you may well disagree.

> *A young, inexperienced director once asked of Charlie Chaplin.*
> *'I want to show a man slipping on a banana skin,*
> *what should I show first, the skin or the man?'*
> *Charlie replied,*
> *'First show the skin, then the man, then show the skin again.*
> *Then show the man stepping over the skin and falling down a manhole!'*

Great living art?

More 'living art' is offered by the actress Shelly Winters, heroine of so many non-naked roles:

> *I think on-stage nudity is disgusting, shameful and damaging to all things American. But if I were 22 with a great body, it would be artistic, tasteful, patriotic and a progressive religious experience.*

Our old friend, 'Phra Farang - An English Monk in Thailand' (Peter Robinson) offers a further insight:

> *There is nothing ultimately ugly about a kidney or spleen. In the same way, there is nothing ultimately beautiful about a bunch of flowers; everything is just the way it is and any attraction or aversion we feel is a personal and relative truth. Of course, at the relative level, if I was a girl I'd much rather be given a bunch of flowers than a bunch of kidneys*

The idea of an object being a 'work of art' emerged, together with the concept of the Artist, in the 15th and 16th centuries in Italy. During the Renaissance, the word Art became known as a collective term encompassing Painting, Sculpture and Architecture, a grouping given currency by the Italian artist and biographer Giorgio Vasari in the 16th century. Subsequently, this grouping was expanded to include Music and Poetry which became known in the 18th century as the 'Fine Arts'. These five fine Arts have formed a nucleus from which have been generally excluded the 'decorative arts' and 'crafts', such as pottery, weaving, metalworking and furniture making, all of which have utility as an end.

Many have, with limited success, attempted to define the essence of a work of art. I rather subscribe to the view propounded by Simon Weil:

> *A work of art has an author and yet, when it is perfect, it has something which is essentially anonymous about it*

Does this mean that if we can easily identify a piece as a Rembrandt or a Constable or a Picasso, that the work is diminished because it is so readily identifiable? Food for thought...

Art lacks a satisfactory definition. It is easier to describe it as the way something is done

The use of skill and imagination in the creation of aesthetic objects, environments, or experiences that can be shared with others (Britannica)

rather than what it is. Thus my argument for including the Charlie Chaplin quotation. But, do you yet agree? Maybe we just accept that each culture and historic moment in time seems to have its own definition of what art is. I certainly remember the pile of red building bricks, masquerading as art, at the National Gallery in London in the 1960's. How the hell could that be art? Or is my mind still not open enough? Huh!

Art is making something out of nothing and selling it.

Frank Zappa (1940 - 1993)

I partially agree with Frank, especially where most of 'Modern Art' is concerned, but I agree even more with Al Capp, who before his death at 70 in 1979 left us with this insight:

Abstract art is a product of the untalented, sold by the unprincipled to the utterly bewildered.

However, we might do well to reflect for a moment on one of these 'modern' artists, Pablo Picasso, perhaps the greatest of them all when, just at the same time as Al Capp was giving us the above wisdom, also reminded us that:

There are painters who transform the sun to a yellow spot, but there are others who with the help of their art and their intelligence, transform a yellow spot into the sun.

He's certainly put me in my place. However, we can always depend on good old Samuel Johnson, living between 1709 and 1784 to provide some balance to the equation.

I passionately hate the idea of being with it; I think an artist has always to be out of step with his time. Skill without imagination is craftsmanship and gives us many useful objects such as wickerwork picnic baskets. Imagination without skill gives us modern art.

Imagination *without* skill! Now there's an interesting debate.

Shakespeare's artist was a fellow called Fuseli and I think he had a point that transcends the ages when he said:

Consider it as the unalterable law of Nature that all your power upon others depends on your own emotions. In order to elicit passion in others the artist must live through the passion himself

Let us allow Oscar to bring our little 'journey into art' to a close as he counsels us:

Diversity of opinion about a work of art shows that the work is new, complex, and vital

Let us then, be generous of heart to all artists, whatever media they use and whatever age they lived in and whatever type of art they presented to a suspicious world and agree with Oscar; for where would we be without Pablo Picasso and DH Lawrence and The Beatles and 'Not the Nine-o-clock News', to name just four artistic mindbenders. Picasso left us with this description of his chosen profession, it takes some thinking about:

Painting is a blind man's profession. He paints not what he sees, but what he feels, what he tells himself about what he has seen

Could a blind man have painted The Mona Lisa's smile? I think not. Could a blind man have painted some of the works of Picasso…? Food for thought!

XXIII

Let's have some fun with a couple of true funnies as we refill our glass:

Kirk Douglas on location in Norway filming 'The Vikings' (circa 1953) tells us of this exchange in his autobiography, 'The Ragman's Son':

> *I was standing one day with a group of the actors, watching a bright sunny sky turn to rain. I said to one of the Norwegian boys who was playing a part in the picture, 'Does it always rain here in Norway?' He said, 'I don't know, I'm only eighteen.'*

I'm terrible at remembering jokes, even the best ones; so I very rarely have been known to repeat one; except the one of the man playing golf with his new bifocals, looking down and seeing the golf-ball as if it were the size of a football and his club face as if it were the size of a cricket bat, thus finding it easy to make pars against his rather threatened opponent; until they came to the 12th and our man could no longer contain himself and had to go behind the bushes to relieve himself. He returned to the green abashed and ashamed; a huge wet patch down the front of his trousers. 'What on earth have you done?' asked his companion. 'Well, it's these new glasses, I took it out to have a pee, thought, - that can't be mine – and put it back in again.'

As GK Chesterton was heard to say:

If a man may not laugh at his own jokes, at whose jokes may he laugh?
May not an architect pray in his own cathedral?

I really love the next one, which I have personally authenticated. It comes from a Ministry of Defence journal of 1949:

The best defence against the Atom bomb is not to be there when it goes off

XXIV

And, finally, as we wind up our journey we debate these words:

The only way to enjoy life is to work. Work is much more fun than fun

This from Noel Coward – playwright, who worked until he was 74, then took his elegant departure from this inelegant world.

William Wrigley Jnr. Possessed a similar view of life as he uttered;

Nothing is so much fun as business.
I do not expect to do anything but work
as long as I can stand up

Interesting, isn't it? If you really enjoy what you are doing, then why taint it with the nomenclature, 'work'; for 'work' denotes some degree of pain, of boredom, of trial, of necessity rather than that of enjoyment. If we open our minds and say, 'what have we taken pleasure in or what do we really enjoy in life?', many times we will remember, with great affection, our triumphs and enjoyment at 'work'. Indeed, for some people, a round of golf may possess more of the normally accepted connotations of 'work' than a productive management team meeting or a business lunch, especially when millions of dollars are being negotiated. A much greater personal satisfaction may transpire from constructing and finalizing a business deal than achieving a few pars during an 18 hole game of golf. So, what does that really tell us? Anything can be seen to be 'work', but if we can view that 'work' as enjoyment, being positive rather than unenthusiastic, then perhaps, many fewer people would so readily be searching for or accepting a mythically 'happy retirement'. For many that do are so often sadly disappointed with their new life. A life that is no longer demanding, interesting or challenging and certainly, not so much fun. Work can really, truly, be the best time of your life! And always remember that:

> *It's not how hard or long you work that matters,*
> *It's how much you get done*

Henry Ford worked pretty hard all of his life, 'any colour you like, as long as it's black' and had a wise word or two to say in respect to effort and reward:

> *The man who will use his skill and imagination to*
> *see how much he can give for a dollar, instead of how*
> *little he can give for a dollar is bound to succeed*

In some ways the converse of this can be so often and readily seen by anyone having worked in the conventional multi-national or even in a reasonably sized company, and was well observed by Austin O'Malley when he wrote:

> *The weaker a man in authority, the stronger his*
> *insistence that all his privileges be acknowledged*

For anyone fortunate enough to have been in the position of mentor to or developer of the latent talent in others and for those that come after us, it is prudent for us to remember and extol, as did Theodore Roosevelt:

> *The best executive is the one who has sense enough to pick*
> *men to do what he wants done and self-restraint enough*
> *to keep from meddling with them while they do it*

Or, as Robert Townsend would have us believe:

When you get right down to it, one of the most important tasks
of a manager is to eliminate his people's excuse for failure

I, like so many others, I suspect, am never quite sure why I am here or what I am supposed to accomplish or, even where my direction should be. Sure, being a Virgo I make lists and plans, then I make lists of those lists and plans of those plans, and I just love doing it, but sometimes I wonder whether Harold Pinter had it absolutely correct in the following line from a play I once acted in, - I can't remember the play or who my character was, but I do remember the line:

I was placed off-centre, and have remained so

This, the story of so many people's lives. Moreover, couple Pinter's thought with one from Epictetus, who, (born as a slave c.55 and living a philosophical life as both a student and a teacher until the ripe old age of 80) gave us the following words that allow us to begin to truly understand the malaise that befuddles the minds of most people; the 'average' of our world:

What deserves your attention most is the last thing to get it

We always do the easiest first, we do what we like the most. When we make our daily 'to do' list we put everything on it, the difficult and the easy and the enjoyable. We say to ourselves 'I'll just do the simple stuff first, get rid of it and then move on to the difficult issues'. The only problem is that, having spent the time doing the easy and enjoyable stuff, there is insufficient time remaining today to do the difficult task, so we add it to tomorrow's list. The circle goes on. It is the exceptional person, the above average achiever who does the difficult first, gets it behind them and then moves on to the easy stuff that rapidly gets done. Thus he completes all. The message is prioritize the difficult stuff first and stick to the priority. But you have to be pretty exceptional to do that. Are you? Are you willing to give it a go?

As John Lennon of The Beatles, once penned:

Life is very short and there's no time for fussing and fighting, my friend

Or as Bernard Mannes Baruch reminds us:

One of the secrets of a long and fruitful life is to forgive
everybody and everything every night before you go to bed

And as A.C. Benson was smart enough to point out:

Readjusting is a painful process, but most off
us need it at one time or another

The ability to readjust demands a certain level of maturity well laced with a strong measure of enthusiasm. Indeed, if we are not enthusiastic about people and events in our lives then we become dull to others and dull to ourselves. Clarence Francis had it right:

You can buy a man's time;
You can buy a man's physical presence at a given place;
You can even buy a measured number of
skilled muscular motions per hour or day;
But you cannot buy enthusiasm.
You cannot buy initiative;
You cannot buy loyalty;
You cannot buy devotion of hearts, minds and souls;
You must have to earn those things.

I hope I'm 'better' at 60 than I was at 30 or 40. But what does 'better' mean and who defines it? As Arnold Bennett, the man from my own home town in the Midlands, would remind us:

Any change, even a change for the better,
is always accompanied by drawbacks and discomforts

Maybe this means that although I may (or you may) be 'better' at the age of 60 than at 30 or 40, we have had to give up something along the way to achieve that 'improvement'. What did I give up? What did *you* give up?

However, we would do well to reflect on what our old friend Cais Petronius had to say, around AD 66:

We tried hard, but it seems that every time we were beginning to form up into teams, we would be reorganized. I was to learn later in life that we tend to meet any new situation by reorganizing and a wonderful method it can be for creating the illusion of progress, while providing confusion, inefficiency and demorilisation.

Toujours la meme chose?

I wonder if Peter Drucker ever read Petronius, he might have saved us all a lot of time, but not made himself quite so much money.

Maybe, George Bernard Shaw had a point, however, when he advised;

When people shake their heads because we are living in a restless age, ask them how they would like to live in a stationary one and do without change

Stronger even is the advice from Andre Malraux:

When man faces destiny, destiny ends and man comes into his own

But growing old, as opposed to becoming 'mature' – whatever that means, - I understand the categorisation when it comes to describing a good wine, but I still struggle to understand what maturity is in people. It's not wisdom; that can be attained at any age; we often hear the phrase, 'he has the wisdom of a child', meant as a compliment. Nor is maturity the act of looking at a beautiful young girl and knowing that you can't have her. No, that's more like desperation! I like to think that maturity is realising that the girl does not want to physically possess you, but that she'd like to spend time with you, over a good dinner and a great wine, to learn from you of life and hope and love and, that you would really enjoy to do this in her company, with no hidden agenda at all.

Mind you, I also think that maturity is refusing to travel economy class, on anything, anywhere.

Maybe I lost the thread of this paragraph, anyway, to start again. As I was saying, before I interrupted myself, 'Growing old' is not something anyone looks forward to. The one-time most popular British actor, Kenneth More, he of 'Reach for the Sky' fame, the story of the legless heroic airman, Douglas Bader; reminds us, in his autobiography, 'More or Less', written some ten years before he succumbed to that dreadful disease, Parkinson's, which was to steal his life away at the age of 67:

> *As Swift put it, 'Every man desires to live*
> *long, but no man would be old'*

He was referring to his great friend and mentor, even a sometime surrogate father, Ronnie Squire who let Kenneth into a personal secret:

> *He had a great fear of living until he was ninety. Two sisters of his*
> *lived to a great age, and they had become so crippled with arthritis*
> *that their hands were like elm twigs, gnarled and lumpy. This was*
> *what Ronnie feared; a slow decline of the faculties, not death itself.*

Ronnie died suddenly, complaining of a headache during dinner with his young wife, the day after he and Kenneth More had enjoyed a sprightly game of golf together. Sadly Kenneth More was intellectually capable of watching as his own faculties declined year after terrible year. Life sometimes, is a real bitch.

On a somewhat brighter note, Lord Glenavy, who was Patrick Campbell's father; in talking of his life, highlighted what may have been felt by many of us, especially if we had the opportunity to reach the top, or even to shine at something, before the commonly accepted age or customary time:

> *The special feature of my progression has been the sustained good luck*
> *which has accompanied it, unsupported by any aims or ambitions on*
> *my part. Practically nothing happened in my life otherwise than I*

would have it happen. In my various occupations I have found myself very briefly near the top of the ladder at an early stage, fear then dictating a prompt retreat. It has left me with the superstition that there was some function or significance which I was being facilitated to discharge but of which I have never been able to conceive

There are so many words that I have read about the need to be positive in life. Positiveness, often through persistence. I remember that for many years my dear Mother kept a blue backed book entitled 'The Power of Positive Thinking' by her bedside and read and re-read it until the cover fell away from the text. Why did she need to do that, I wonder? Did she receive profound support from the words within, or was there a deeper darker reason? I think I'll leave that where it is. Brian Mayfield-Smith, an easy man to understand, although not an easy man to know, had this to say about positivism and persistence in his autobiography, 'The Outsider – A Personal Journey'

> *If you adopt a positive and persistent attitude in pursuing your ideals and dreams, then things can come out very well; that once you give up, that is the finish of it, but that <u>nothing</u> is finished with you personally until you make the decision to give up, that even though you might be getting a beating, you are not beaten until you give up.*

Not terribly eloquent, but absolutely to the point.

I rather like and agree with, as perhaps we all must, the thoughts of Franklin P. Adams when he renewed our faith in ourselves by stating:

> *There must be a day or two in a man's life when he is the precise age for something important*

Have you had that age, that moment yet? Do you indeed know whether you have had it?

I think the barrister (obviously not autobiographical) in one of the brilliant John Mortimer stories, had a wonderful such moment:

A barrister, an experienced and effective defender in criminal trials on
a good day, rises to his feet in the Old Bailey. This is not a good day.
His life is in tatters. A mental storm, long threatened by gathering black
clouds of depression, is about to burst inside his head. He has had a liquid
lunch in the pub across the road and, although a large and weighty man,
he sways and creaks like a tree in a high wind. It is a quarter past two
in the afternoon and he feels a strong disposition to sleep overcome him.
'Members of the jury' – his voice is deep and comes softly at first, the
half-audible hint of approaching thunder – 'this is the point in the case
at which I am supposed to make a reasoned and persuasive speech on
behalf of the accused. That will be followed by an unbiased summing-
up from the learned judge, and you will then retire and come to a just
decision. But' – here comes a great sigh and then a louder, clearer burst
of thunder – ' as I am far too drunk to make a reasoned and persuasive
speech, and as the judge has never given an unbiased summing-up
in his entire career, and as you look far too stupid to come to a just
verdict, I shall sit down.' He does so and, happy at last, closes his eyes.

Maybe W H Auden, who graced this world with his erudition until
1973, had it entirely right when he stated:

We are here on Earth to do good to others. What
the others are here for, I don't know.

JG Farrell in 'The Siege of Krishnapur', had this wise reminder of
our worth to others:

Fleury was confronted, as he toiled clumsily with the sponging
rod in the dust and smoke, with a simple fact about human
nature which he had never considered before: nobody is superior
to anyone else, he may only be better at doing a specific thing

I realize that a high majority of my quotes have been made with
the male 'he' rather than the female 'her', - but that's how they were
written. So I here and now humbly apologise to all the feminists
that may have got this far in my book. One day someone will write a
similar book to this and there will ONLY be quotations from women
about women.

And, of course, I really, really don't go along with Dame Edith Evans who proclaimed:

> *When a woman behaves like a man, why*
> *doesn't she behave like a nice man?*

Now, Dame Edith, where on earth have you been living? Ah yes, on Earth.

But if not on Earth, then do we still have a problem, highlighted by one salutary thought from John Oliver Hobbs:

> *All the angels we know anything about are men*

And even more poignantly, from Adrienne E. Gusoff (whom I would liked to have had the pleasure to meet, for reasons that shall become obvious; just for debate, you understand)

> *Any woman who thinks the way to a man's heart is through*
> *his stomach is aiming about 10 inches too high.*

Becoming less smutty; when I read for the first time, some years ago, the next quotation from Sir Peter Ustinov, talking about his third wife in his autobiography, 'Dear Me' it struck a real chord in me. As I read it again today, the chord reverberates even stronger:

> *A perfect woman could have no personality. Helene (A?) is a harmony*
> *of delightful imperfections, which is the most flattering thing I could*
> *say about anyone. I only hope my imperfections seem half as delightful*
> *to her. It is so easy to take if there is someone with so much to give.*
> *She has made me into something approaching the man I once hoped*
> *to be, privately and secretly. She has the kind of sense of humour*
> *which invests trouble with proportion and happiness with grace*

Or from…(guess)…

> *Every woman is a rebel, and usually in wild revolt against herself*

Yes, Oscar Wilde, - how did he know and say so many wise and wonderful things? Where did the genius come from to allow him to string simple words together into something overwhelmingly accurate and profound, as he did when reflecting on the differences in the motivation of humans ensconced in a wicked prison for straight sins:

Two men look out through the same bars, one
sees the mud, the other the stars

Always, but always, - see the stars, and your life will become positive and beautiful, maybe also attempt to be similar to Churchill when you look for, find and then cherish your ultimate partner, agree with him and protect what you have when he says:

I am easily satisfied by the very best

Or learn from a namesake, Charles Churchill, who advised:

If you mean to profit, learn to please

Or with Thomas Fuller who simply says:

Good is not good where better is expected

But is life truly like that in our 21st Century? Or is it rather more accurately and more depressingly described by Stirling Silliphant, in 'Silver Star' – when he says:

The most difficult issue any human being – man, woman or
child, - faces in this twentieth century (now twenty-first, but
the issue is wretchedly the same) *is to try to evolve some sort*
of workable personal guideline through the shitstorm of endemic
violence and its unremitting clutch on the innocents of the world

And be prepared to forgive. I'll never forget a line from that sympathetic movie 'On Golden Pond' when Katherine Hepburn said, speaking to her vexed daughter (Jane Fonda) about her (real-life as well) father, Katherine's ever grumpy husband, played by Henry Fonda:

> *Sometimes you have to look hard at a person.-*
> *He's just trying his best to find his way, just as you are*

Holbrook Jackson put it slightly differently and perhaps less positively:

> *Don't try to convert the elderly person:*
> *- circumvent him*

Robert Owen, equally as wise, offers:

> *Never argue: repeat your assertion*

A somewhat contrary statement to the above thoughts come from the highly opinionated and never shyly retiring Sigmund Freud, who once proclaimed to the world:

> *I have examined myself thoroughly and come to the*
> *conclusion that I don't need to change much*

Well, at least the guy had balls. And, maybe, a soul mate in Mark Twain who admitted:

> *I like criticism, but it must be my way*

Or John Steinbeck, who managed to work through three wives in his lifetime, 1902-1968, no doubt they contributed to his raw reminiscence that:

> *No one wants advice – only corroboration*

Three times?

More interestingly, perhaps, is an 'in character' reaction by Steinbeck, who not only abrogated advice, but also claimed the Nobel Prize for literature in 1962 for his, somewhat difficult to read but always passionate and intensely interesting novels; maturing from the first, 'Tortilla Flat', through 'Of Mice and Men' to the outstanding social chronicle entitled 'The Grapes of Wrath'. In 1957 Salinas (his home town) contemplated naming North Salinas High School after Steinbeck. Steinbeck wrote a now-famous letter to a Californian staff member against the idea, saying he didn't want school children to curse his name:

'If the city of my birth should wish to perpetuate my name clearly but harmlessly, let it name a bowling alley after me or a dog track or even a medium price, low-church brothel; but a school!'

Mr. Steinbeck died at the age of 66, as, almost, did Horace Walpole; he too was not renowned as the cheeriest of people, but he certainly had something when he said (in 1774 at the age of 67 – which was actually pretty old in those times):

Old age is no such uncomfortable thing, if one gives oneself up to it with good grace

Don't you just love it when someone really hits the nail directly on the head:

So too, did Roy Hattersley in his autobiography 'Who Goes Home'. Roy was deputy leader of the Labour party under Neil Kinnock. He was an astute politician who for 30 years was always close to the very top of British politics but never made it to Leader of the Opposition or to Prime Minister. He just didn't want it enough. But, in his eminently readable autobiography, written at the age of sixty, just as he was leaving politics to become a full-time writer, he advised us, from his vantage point of age that:

There is no point in being sixty if you remain as arrogant as you were when you were thirty-five

Sadly, so many of us still do, or, worse, become even more arrogant. There is an old Italian proverb that bodes well for us all to remember in those moments of self imposed passion, especially when argument is spurious:

It is a good answer which knows when to stop

The Chinese are also pretty good at old proverbs or sayings, if they can ever stand still for a moment in their rush to become Americans:

If you are patient in one moment of anger,
You will escape a hundred days of sorrow

Alexandre Dumas had something similar to say on the same theme, but his words were even smarter than the sayings from China or Italy. He astutely points out:

There is nothing more galling to angry people than the
coolness of those on whom they wish to vent their spleen

Remember it! Remember it next time you get yourself into one of those brainless emotive discussions or into an absurd road-rage situation. Remember it and you will triumph. Or perhaps, you can top it with recalling what astute John W. Raper (who? – well, at least he has an elementary school in Cleveland Ohio named after him) tells us:

There is no sense in having an argument with a man so
stupid he doesn't know you have the better of him

Changing pace and a little direction, let us consider the next, more personalized yet perfectly fitting quotation as we journey along life's pathway; it is from Albert Camus in his novel 'The Fall'

Alas, after a certain age, every man is responsible for his face

That, I find to be just a little bit scary, but when I think of the many blotchy, sunken eyed and pithy faces I've met along life's highway, I cannot take exception to his point.

I can't remember who is responsible for the next quote, but it fits well into this our final chapter as we analyze ourselves and how we have lived hitherto and how we are now going to live for the remainder of our lives:

One day as a lion is worth a lifetime as a mouse

Prophetically, let us momentarily place John Lennon with Cicero, with a different bent upon this thing called life and remember his words:

Life is what happens to you when you are making other plans

A thought echoed by William Ellery Channing who would have us remember:

We must not waste time in devising means.
It is better to plan less and do more.

And, never ever despair if you are not such a good planner or doer, Oscar didn't, even when contemplating his own death, (at the tender age of 46) he viewed the prospect, not without some amusement when he said:

I suppose I shall have to die beyond my means

And what's so bad about that? He did. And what richness he left us with.

But where, you may ask, is Willy Shakespeare in this book of reminiscences and quotations? The truth is that as he so easily fills an entire book by himself, I have left until almost the end of my meanderings around life, just a very few of his wisest words:

This above all, – to thine own self be true, – for it follows as
the night the day, thou canst not then be false to any man

Polonius in 'Hamlet'

Finally, please dear reader, always remember:

Zog nit keynmol az du geyst dem letztn veg

Which translated, means:

Never say that you are walking your final road

From Misha Defonseca, in her autobiography, 'Surviving with Wolves'

Finally, finally, please dear reader, always, always remember:

No one is so old that he does not think he could live another year

This came from Cicero in 44 BC – he lived one more year!!

ROCK ON!!

Or, if you really don't want to 'Rock On', then remember, at our age, what E.V. Lucas so pithily advised:

One of the most adventurous things left us is to go to bed.
For no one can lay a hand on our dreams

Goodnight all!

"Goodnight all"

From Tweedledum and Tweedledee

Printed in the United Kingdom
by Lightning Source UK Ltd.
125044UK00001B/180/A